Marta Chiodera

Chiavenna, Italy

1810-1886

MARTA CHIODERA

FROM ITALY TO ARGENTINA

A Family Story

THE HISTORY OF THE

PEREGO-GANDOLLA FAMILY

Marta Stiefel Ayala, PhD
San Diego, California

ISBN: 978-1-329-29480-6

Imprint: Lulu.com

TABLE OF CONTENTS

PHOTOS

INTRODUCTION

This is the story of the Perego-Gandolla family which captures their history as far back as we could trace it while incorporating historical photos and texts acquired during our research. This project began in 2008 during our first major family reunion in Córdoba, Argentina. While visiting, we started talking about locating more information about the Perego-Gandolla side of the family, as Caroso had been so successful in searching and finding so much about the Stiefel side of the family. One of the great discoveries was a wonderful suitcase, full of old photos, that our cousin Tatana had inherited from Tía Ofelia, her mother, who inherited it from Abuela María. Caroso and I scanned many of the photos, mainly those from Italy and particularly those from Chiavenna, in the hopes of being able to identify them someday. Another surprise was to find a letter from Olympia Aureggi from Milano to Tatana written in 1988 where she was talking about a "Marta Perego" from San Diego who was looking for me.

When we returned to San Diego, I went back to the letter again; it was hard to read because it was in Italian. We thought that Marta Perego would no longer be in San Diego, after so many years, but just in case, we looked in the phone book and there was an M. Perego. We called that phone number, and it was Marta! She is the daughter of Giovanni Perego, and she is a researcher in molecular biology at the Scripps Institute in San Diego. By then, we had already decided to travel to Italy with my daughter, Suchi and my granddaughters, Nastassia and Maya, daughters of Emiliano and Carlos, respectively. Coincidentally, Marta Perego was going to travel to Chiavenna at the same time, so we were able to get together at the house of her father, Giovanni Perego. She served as a translator and guide to the city, and we were able to have long conversations with her dad. He took us to the cemetery where part of the Perego and Chiodera families are buried. We also toured the town of Chiavenna and surrounding areas. He showed us some photos, documents, the house, and the furniture that have been in the family for generations. After Chiavenna, we went to Milano, where another part of the family lives: Olympia Aureggi (daughter of Margherita Perego and Alessandro Aureggi) with her husband Francesco Ariatta, her daughter Margherita, and her grandchildren, Olympia and Francesco. We talked a lot about the family because Olympia remembered all the relatives in great detail. She was in contact with Abuela María for many years and Abuela María had visited her in Chiavenna. Margherita showed us the castle of the Count Sforza in Milano, to whom we are related. Olympia promised to help us with data research and family stories.

When we returned to San Diego, I made two packages with the updated family tree with copies of the unidentified photos and sent them to Don Giovanni and Olympia. We communicated with them often trying to clarify information, get new data, and identify the unidentified photos. Meanwhile, I continued to visit the Mormons' Genealogical Research Center to research information about births and deaths in Bellagio and Chiavenna and locate the foreign passengers' arrival ledgers to Argentina. At the center, I also searched the Internet and use borrowed films from the main research archive located in Salt Lake City, Utah. Unfortunately, for those two regions, the information in those databases doesn't go back far enough, only until the mid-1800s. In this document, you will find some information about Chiavenna and Bellagio, the birthplaces of our family on Abuela María's side. I included many identified photos from Italy and of our family members in Argentina. The last part of this book includes a descendant chart, letters, copies of some birth and death certificates, copies of Mormon database records, and family stories that I hope we can expand in the future. This was a collaborative effort from many people and it's a never-ending project. There's always one more fact, one more photo, another unidentified relative, another surprise. I hope this effort will not end here and that this book, along with our other publications about the Stiefel family, continue to grow with ongoing family contributions.

7

PHOTO 1 – THE PANDORA SUITCASE, WHERE SO MANY
PHOTOGRAPHIC TREASURES WERE FOUND

PHOTO 2 – OSCAR (CAROSO) AND MARTA
SCANNING PHOTOS AT TATANA'S HOUSE

THE PANDORA SUITCASE

This is the suitcase that started everything! One day, my brother Oscar (Caroso) was visiting my cousin Tatana, and as it generally happens when our family gets together, they started talking about the family: old stories, new stories, some gossip, good memories, forgettable incidents and so on. Caroso mentioned that we had very few pictures of the family from the old countries, that is, Italy and Germany. Well, to his surprise, my cousin Tatana appeared with a very old, battered suitcase which had belonged to Abuela María and was passed down from mother to daughter until it landed at Tatana's house. When Caroso opened the suitcase, he could not believe what was inside: old pictures, letters, postcards, souvenirs, and what not. He spent hours that day looking at the pictures and on the next visit to her house, he brought a scanner and a computer and started scanning the pictures there, since she would not let go of the suitcase.

All this gave him the push to start working on the family tree and he has been doing that for several years; first researching the German side of the family and then working on the Italian side. He then began organizing family reunions. One of those years, he took me to Tatana's house, and we continued scanning and identifying photos in preparation for the next year's reunion. Many of the photos we couldn't identify, so it became my job to make copies and send them to Italy hoping the family could identify them.

In the photo above, you can see the suitcase, and in the photo below, you can see my brother Oscar (Caroso), me (Marta), the computer, and the scanner. My cousin Tatana is just outside the picture (wearing black boots).

During the summer of 2009, I traveled to Italy with my daughter, Suchi and two of my granddaughters, Maya and Nastassia. We met with part of the family, the Ariattas, in Chiavenna and Milano, took many pictures of the tombstones, the village, and the family. It was a great trip!

PHOTO 3 - DINNER IN MILANO WITH THE
ARIATTA FAMILY, JUNE 28, 2009.

9

PHOTO 4 - CHIAVENNA

VIA DOLTZINO

RIO MERA

PALACIO SALIS

C
H
I
A
V
E
N
N
A

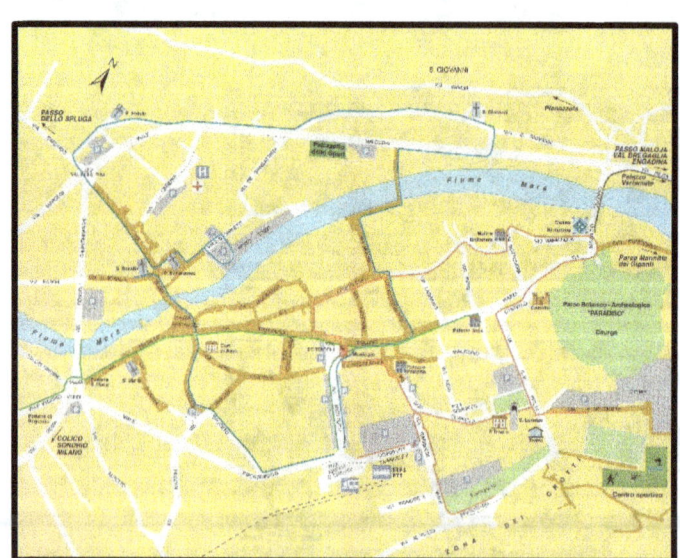

MAP OF CHIAVENNA

PORTÓN DE SANTA MARÍA

A BRIEF HISTORY OF CHIAVENNA

The city of Chiavenna is located at the foothills of the Raetianos Alps, where the valley of the river Liro (Valley of Splurga) and the valley of the Mera River (Valley of Bregaglia) come together. The center of the town is located in a narrow and deep ravine formed by the Rio Mera. The buildings around Chiavenna are at the bottom, on the fluvial cones or on the terraces that interrupt the steep slopes. These slopes are covered with materials displaced by the landslides that occurred after the glaciers melted about 10,000 to 12,000 years ago. The Chiavenesque poet Giovanni Bertacchi wrote that the name Chiavenna "with a slow and closed sound, seems to reflect the shadow of the valleys where it hides, behind the walls, hills and cliffs that embrace with savage intimacy the soul of its inhabitants and that nourishes its faith and its indelible memories". The Romans called it "Clavenla". This name appears on a military map of the third century and on the route of Antonino, in the following century. The "Diácono" Paolo Warnefrido, in the "History of the Longobardos", which he wrote at the end of this century, recalls that Ausprando, the King of the Longobardos, pursued by Ariperto II, escapes to "Clavenna", by Chur before arriving in Bavaria. The origin of the name "Clavenna" comes from long ago. By 1200s it was already linked to "clavem" (key) and in 1260 the commune commissioned ten white linen flags with a key made of silk appliqued to the middle of the flags. In 1616, Giovanni Guler, of Grigione, introducing the county of Chiavenna in his post "Raetia", notes: "... whose name comes from the word "key". In fact, the castle of Chiavenna, which gave its name to the village and the surrounding territory, "in the past [...] was a kind of key that closed the way to foreign people." This etymology is interesting, but not very convincing. Now, it seems that the etymology comes from the Mediterranean root "clava", which would have to do with "alluvial cone," that is, alluvial deposits at the end of a valley. This theory may be true, because Chiavenna was born from the deposits of the river Mera, according to geological evidence. The name of this Alpine village is the same as that of the river that flows into the Po, near Piacenza and which has given the name to two towns: Chiavenna Rocchetta and Chiavenna Landi. The Roman "Clavenna" was a station of importance on the routes that led to the passes to reach the borders of the empire in Rezia and Norico; especially when Milan became one of the capitals of the empire. For this period, documentation is scarce. There are several archaeological finds that came to light during excavations to lay the foundations of buildings, drainage, telephone cables, and power lines. These discoveries were made between the beds of the Mera and the Pratogiano rivers. Very little is known from the period following the fall of the Roman Empire. Christianity is spread; under the Longobardos, Chiavenna becomes one of the most important trading and customs centers of the empire. In the 10th century, the King Itálico granted the bishop of Como the tax collection of Chiavenna. Under the influence of the Duchy of Svevia, the people in power were interested in supporting Emperor Frederick in the fight against the communes of Lombardy. He gave them to his friend, Guiberto Grasso, for the creation of the abbot of Sta. María di Dona (Pratal). At the end of the winter of 1176, Barbarossa met in Chiavenna with his cousin Enrico, El León, Duke of Baviara and Sassonia, to obtain support for his military campaigns in Italy. During the 1200s, the struggles between the feudal families of Como continued, and this had negative repercussions on the valley. In 1335, the Visconti family of Milan became monarchs of the Valchiavenna Valley, which they placed under the Balbiani family of Varenna. The Sforza family followed the Viscontis. In 1486, they tried to take possession of the southern valleys; burned down the village, looted it and returned to their territory after losing many ducats. Milan realized that the northern borders were at risk and took steps to strengthen the most important centers. Chiavenna was fenced off with walls, erected between 1488 and 1497, along 2 kilometers, with fourteen large towers and three gates (to Milan-Como, Val S. Giacomo and the Bregaglia Valley). The project was planned by Ambrogio Ferrari; also present were the architect Giovanni Antonio Amedeo and Leonardo da Vinci, who remembers the Chiavenna Valley in its "Atlantic Code". Ludovico el Moro was followed by the French; but because they did not leave very good memories, the villagers had great relief when the Grigioni, in 1512, took possession of Valchiavenna, Valtellina and the region around Bormio. The name of the Republic of the Three Alliances (which now corresponds to the Swiss canton of Grigioni) lasted until 1797, with a pause between 1620 and 1639.

The 1500s were for Chiavenna a period of prosperity, at least for the wealthy families, who invested their capitals in the construction of palaces, along the main and secondary roads, with warehouses on the first floor and elegant quarters upstairs.

The Grigioni supported the Protestant Reformation and imposed religious tolerance for Catholics and the reformed. Religious and lay people who left Italy to escape the Inquisition, took refuge in Chiavenna. Among them was Francisco Negri de Bassano, who opened a humanist school, Augustin Mainardi who founded the reformist church S. María del Patarino, Ludovico Castelvetro, of Modena, who died in Chiavenna, and many others. Along with the immigrates there were also Chiavenna natives who became Protestants. The Reformation built three churches to conduct its services. The relationship with Catholics was not always easy, especially since Protestants had the support of the dominant authority. In Valtellina, in 1620, protests broke out that resulted in the massacre of hundreds of Protestants. The political reasons were masked by religious reasons, although it is not always possible to distinguish between the two causes. There were no massacres in Valchiavenna. In the following years, until the Milan treaty of 1639, there were several military occupations as the Adda and Mera valleys, backed by the great powers (France, Venice, and Spain) were a strategic region of great importance. The Lanzquenets, on their way to Mantova, were arrested in Milan and they carried the plague, which killed about a third of the population, devastating the area and reducing the inhabitants to starvation.

With the Treaty of Milan of 1639, Chiavenna was again granted to the Grigioni. One of the clauses of the treaty established that the only religion admitted in those territories was Catholic and prohibited residency for Protestants. During this period, many of the sacred buildings, legally granted to Protestants, were restructured. In Chiavenna, the convents of the Franciscans and the Agostines were founded; the first where the Patarino church had been and the second, next to the church of St. Pietro. In the 1700s, frictions between the governors and the emperor's subjects were aggravated, as the former imposed a commercial monopoly, and this marked the end of the domination of the Grigione. The peoples of Valtellina and Valchiavenna, in 1797, called for and obtained their annexation to the republic of Cisalpina. The Grigioni, due to internal conflicts, had accepted the ex-colony as the Fourth Alliance, provoking Napoleon's suspicions, who had decided on the annexation to the Cisalpine. In 1814, the Griogino's efforts to recover Chiavenna were thwarted. The Congress of Vienna established that Valtellina and Valchiavenna be annexed to the reign of Lombardy-Veneto. The fate of the Mera Valley was now definitely linked to Lombardy. Under the Austrians' administration many major administrative reforms were carried out, economic activity was increased due to the new infrastructures, especially related to the brewing and textile industry. In 1859, Chiavenna came under the reign of Sardinia, which in 1861 was the reign of Italy. Then began a period of economic crippling due to customs policies; the collapse of the local economy occurred with the development of the passes of Fréjus, S. Gottardo and Sempione, strategic points for transportation between Pedania and the valleys of the Alps.

OLD BUILDINGS AND SHALE ROOFS IN CHIAVENNA

A BRIEF HISTORY OF BELLAGIO

Lake Como, with its blue waters surrounded by gardens and forests and backed by the snow-capped Alps, generates strong feelings. Romance, inspiration, even soft melancholy~ these are the emotions that for centuries the lake had motivated poets (Lord Byron), novelist (Stendhal), Composers (Verdi and Rossini) and many more visitors, queens, such as the deposed Caroline de Brunswick, whom George IV of England exiled there for her depraved ways; or to modern travelers who slide over the blue waters on steam boats or, these days, the rich and famous such as George Clooney, who owns a villa there.

Besides its suggestive power, Lake Como is a nice place to rest. Less than an hour from Milano by train or car, its sparkling waters and its deep and green coasts provide a wonderful respite from modern and urban life. It is understood why Lake Como served as a backdrop for romantic scenes in "Star Wars II: Clones Attack"~ one of the very few movie scenes that were not created digitally. We suppose that even George Lucas realized that Como was a place of such a beauty that he did not need to tweak the images.

Bellagio is known as one of the most beautiful cities in Italy. Nestled amid cypress groves and green gardens, its ancient terracotta buildings climb from the lake promenade along cobblestoned and stepped streets. Although Bellagio is a very popular place for visitors from the Milanese region who spend a day of rest, and the British and Americans who come to relax for a week or two, the city has generally not been overwhelmed by tourism. One of Bellagio's famous gardens surrounds the Villa de Melzi, built by Francesco Melzi, a friend of Napoleon and an official of his Republic. The villa was the retreat of Franz Liszt and is now home to a distinguished family from Lombardy; the public is allowed to visit its large and beautiful gardens and fountains including a pavilion where a collection of Egyptian sculptures is on display. Another famous garden in Bellagio is that of the Villa Serbelloni, occupying land owned by Pliny the Younger, which is now in the hands of the Rockefeller Foundation.

Bellagio, called "The Pearl of Lake Como, was already famous in Roman times. Its beautiful geographical position and strategically important location have created its history. It is believed, from archaeological evidence, that there was human presence in the vicinity of Bellagio in the Paleolithic period (about 30,000 years ago), but only until the 7th century appeared a "castellum" on a promontory, a place of worship and trade, which served the many small villages of the lake. But it was in Roman times that Lake Como, called Larius by the Romans, began its important role. The Romans introduced the olive and laurel trees and that we still find in abundance today on the shores of the lake. Pliny the Younger (1st century) describes in a letter the long periods he spent in his village of Bellagio, during which he devoted himself not only to study and writing but also to hunting and fishing. With the occupation of the Longobardos, Bellagio was more fortified. In 744, King Luitprando settled there.

It is believed that Bellagio was a free municipality and a seat of a court by the year 1100 and that his dependence on Como was merely formal. However, Bellagio's strategic position was very important for the city of Como, which had no tolerance for these autonomic tendencies. Bellagio, therefore, had to suffer more than one foray from Como and fought fierce naval battles against this neighbor. In 1154, under Frederick Barbarossa, Bellagio was forced to swear allegiance and pay homage to Como. Towards the end of the thirteenth century, Bellagio, who had participated in numerous wars on the side of the Gibelinos, (pro-empire party), became the property of the Visconti and was integrated into the Duchy of Milan. To transport all guests to the festivities for the marriage of Bianca Maria Sforza and Emperor Maximilian I, on December 6, 1493, 32 highly decorated ships were needed. In 1535, when Francesco II Sforza, the last Duke of Milan, died, they began, in Lombardy and on the lands of Lake Larius, two centuries of onerous Spanish rule, during which time the book "Sposi de promess" (La Prometida) was written.

An important and evocative testimony of Spanish domination is the staircase called "Derta" built in this period that leads from the Guggiate district to the Suira district. In 1533, Francesco Sfondrati bought the feud of Bellagio and for more than 200 years the Sfondrati family was the most important reference point for Bellagio and its history. All the progress and events of the city were associated with this family. In the Bellagio of these times, favored by the ideal position for transport and trade, several small industries were established among which candle production was particularly remarkable and silk production along with its corollaries, silkworm breeding and blackberry cultivation. With the death of Carlo Sfondrati in 1788, Bellagio's fiefdom passed into the hands of the illustrious Serbelloni family. At the end of the eighteenth century, Alessandro Serbelloni spent 929,622 euros (equivalent to today's euros) on improvements to his private park, when a worker's daily salary was less than one hundredth of a euro per day.

During the brief Napoleonic period, the port of Bellagio assumed a strategic and military importance and an event, apparently of secondary importance, channeled the fate of Bellagio towards the following two centuries: the decision of Count Francesco Melzi, Duke of Lodi and Vice President of the Republic of Cisalpina to establish his summer house there. Count Melzi proceeded to build on the west bank, near Loppia, a magnificent villa. This attracted to the area the top of the Milanese nobility and the promontory was transformed into an elegant and refined court. Roads were built for the carriages, first to link the villas and palaces, then to the city center and finally the provincial road Erba-Bellagio was completed. The fame of the small town on the splendid lake would be known far from the confines of Lombardo-Veneto: even Emperor Francis I of Austria visited it in 1816 and returned in 1825 to stay in the Villas Serbelloni, Trotti and Melzi.

In 1838, Bellagio received with all the honors Emperor Fernando I, archduke Raneri and Minister Mettemich, who arrived there from Varenna on the ship "Lario", the first steamship on the lake, having been launched in 1826. Bellagio was one of the most frequented towns by the nobility of Lombardy and the constructions of beautiful villas, gardens, and luxury shops began. Tourists crowded the roads and space was limited, so it was decided to tear down the old port that reached the portal in order to build a wider square. Tourism had already become the main economic resource of the town of Bellagio and from this period onwards Bellagio's history coincides with that of its hotels.

The first was hotel Bellagio, founded in 1825 with the renovation of the former hospitality house of Abbondio Genazzini, and which was later converted into the first large hotel on the lake, the Genazzini Hotel. Following the example of these forerunners, several splendid hotels were built in the space of a few years, many of which continue to function and frequently remain in the hands of the same families who founded them. Some of these are: Hotel Firenze, built on the former house of Captain del Lario in 1870, Grand Hotel Bellagio, now the Grand Hotel Villa Serbelloni, opened in 1872.

In 1888, the three largest hotels, Genazzini, Grande Bretagne and Grand Hotel Bellagio, for the first time, introduced electric light to replace gas lighting, and after that many patrician houses followed. During the 19th century, when many nobles stayed in Bellagio hotels, they often rented entire flats and used some rooms only to display their clothes on the beds. Senator Gary Hart of the USA loved his stay in Bellagio so much that he used the place as the basis for a spy novel in which a secret agent hides in a Bellagio hotel. In Las Vegas, Steve Wynn, the President of Mirage Resorts, has built a hotel-casino named Bellagio, declaring it to be the most romantic hotel in the world. The hotel has 37 floors, 3,421 rooms and a staff of 8,000. The entire complex occupies a space of 83 hectares and includes an artificial lake with fountains, dozens of gardens and a "village" with small boutiques and shops that resemble those of the city of Lake Como. Bellagio also saw the birth of 6 world rowing champions: Alberto Belgeri, Enrico Gandolla, Igor Pescialli, Franco Sancassani, Daniele Gilardoni, and Elisabetta Sancassani; first European water-skiing speed champion: David Conti; first European football champion: Giacomo Cranchi ("Pacio"); first European beach volleyball champion: Laura Bruschini. "Bellagio was one of the first Italian tourist center that became truly international and never degenerated into a 'tourist machine'.

VIEWS OF
LAKE COMO
AND
BELLAGIO

MAP OF CHIAVENNA, BELLAGIO, AND MILANO

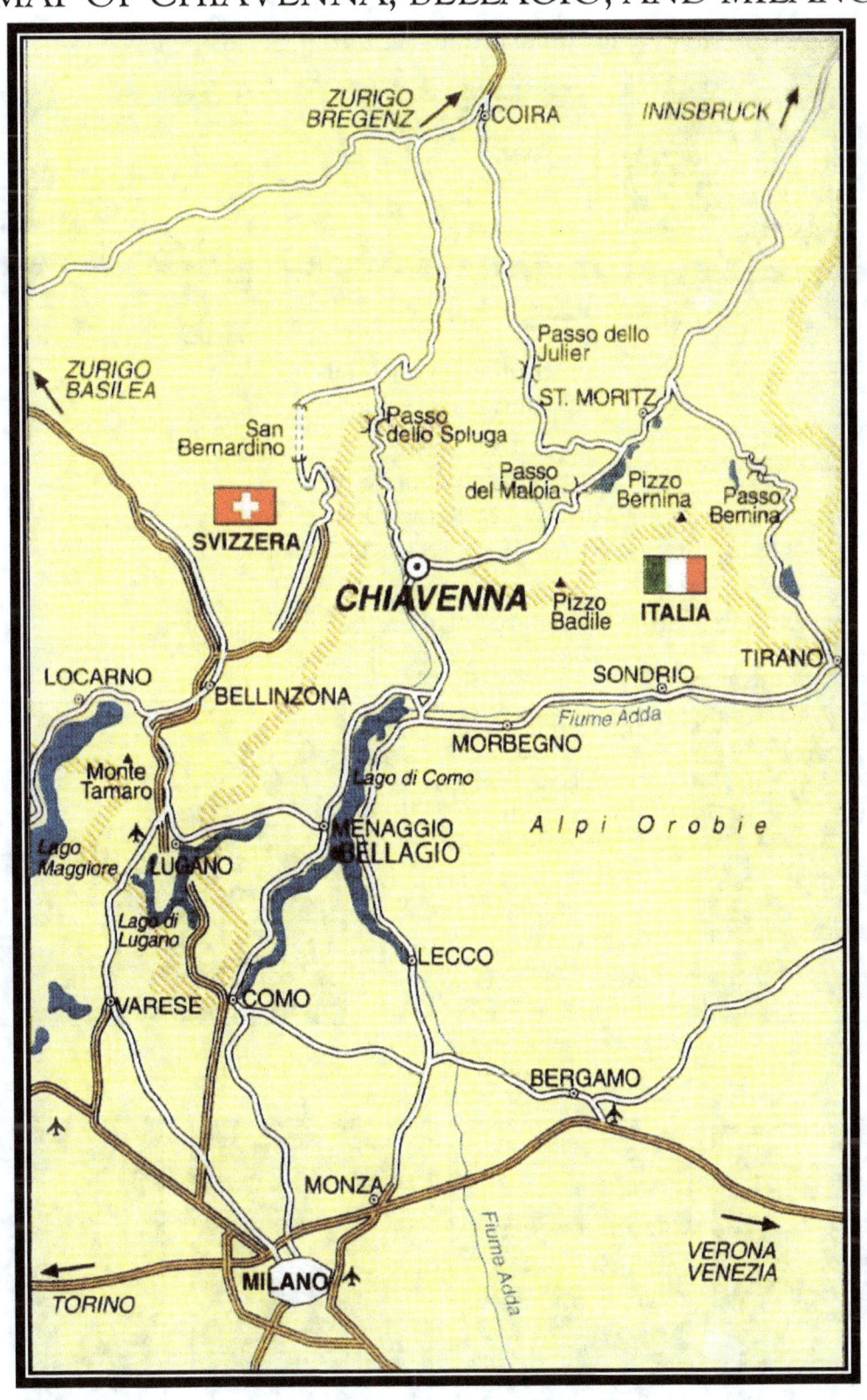

PEREGOS' TOMBS
Caterina Perego de Gandolla Tomb in Carlos Pellegrini

Inscription on the tomb
Catalina P. de Gandolla
Q.E.P.D
Nació el 25 de abril de 1847
Murió el 14 de marzo de 1895
Sus deudos le rinden este homenaje

Chiavenna Cemetery and Perego-Riva Mausoleum

Inscription on the tomb

Alla cara memoria
di
Giovanni Perego
Morto il 16 dicembre 1863
Nell'eta d'anni 55
Marta Chiodera Perego
Morta il 12 febbraio 1886
Nell'eta d'anni 76

SHIELD AND PLAQUE ON CHIODERA'S TOMB
CHURCH OF SAN LORENZO IN CHIAVENNA

PHOTO 5 - CHIODERA'S
FAMILY SHIELD

PHOTO 6 - PLAQUE UNDER
SHIELD

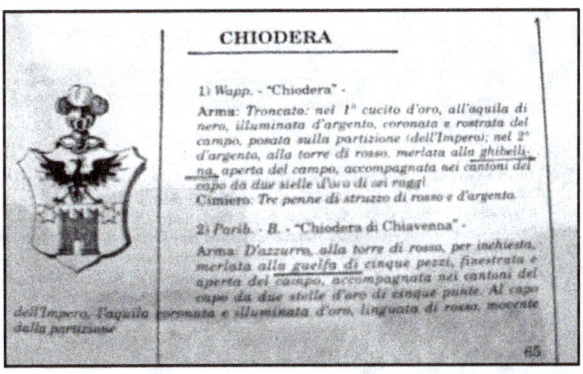

Explanation of the shield

Translation of the Explanation "Chiodera"

Armor: truncated: in the 1st embroidery in gold, the black eagle, illuminated in silver, crowned, with a beak on the field, resting on the Empire's division. In the 2nd, of silver, a red tower, a wall, open to the field, accompanied on the top, by two stars with 6 points. Three Ostrich feathers in red and gold.

Chiodera di Chiavenna

Armor: blue, with red tower, with a flat wall in 5 pieces, with an open window to the field, together with head cantons and 2 stars with 5 points. On top of the Empire, a crowned eagle illuminated in gold, with a pink tongue, on top of the division.

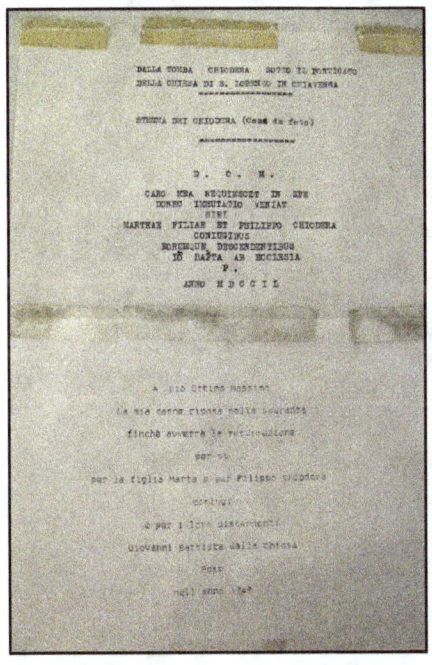

Plaque's Translation

To all forgiving God, my body rests on the hope that until the resurrection arrives, by you, for my daughter Marta and for Filippo Chiodera, spouses, and their descendants.

Giovanni Batista Della Chiesa

Placed in 1749

19

GANDOLLA-PEREGO FAMILY

PHOTO 7 - CATERINA (CATALINA)
PEREGO DE GANDOLLA

PHOTO 8 - ARISTIDES GANDOLLA

PHOTO 9 – CATERINA, MARÍA, ARÍSTIDES, AND DUILIO GANDOLLA

LA ABUELA MARIA
THROUGHOUT HER LIFETIME

PHOTO 11 - LA ABUELA MARÍA AT
VILLA DEL LAGO

PHOTO 10 - MARÍA GANDOLLA DE STIEFEL, CARLOS H.
STIEFEL AND OTILIA STIEFEL

21

LOS ABUELOS AT ESTANCIA ALTO
ALEGRE, PASCANAS, PROVINCIA
DE CÓRDOBA

PHOTO 12 - MARÍA GANDOLLA DE STIEFEL AND CARLOS
H. STIEFEL EN LA MOTO NAVE IGUAZÚ

PHOTO 13 - ABUELA MARÍA WITH RAÚL. FROM RIGHT TO LEFT: LITA, JORGE, ENRIQUE, ISABELITA, CARLITOS (CHINGO), AND YIYI IN ALTO ALEGRE

PHOTO 14 - OFELIA, OTILIA, WITH OCTAVIO, ORMANDO AND OSCAR ON TRICYCLE

OTILIA ENRIQUETA, OLDEST
CHILD OF MARIA G. DE STIEFEL
AND CARLOS HENRY STIEFEL
SHE BECAME MOTHER
SUPERIOR IN THE ORDER OF
LAS ADORATRICES.

PHOTO 15 - CARLOS, MARÍA, OTILIA AND
OCTAVIO

24

OFELIA CARMEN STIEFEL, SECOND DAUGHTER OF MARIA GANDOLLA DE STIEFEL AND CARLOS HENRY STIEFEL

PHOTO 17 - OFELIA AND MARÍA ISABEL CASTELLANOS

PHOTO 16 - TÍA OFELIA AND LITA

PHOTO 18 - TÍA OFELIA AS WE ALL REMEMBER HER

25

ORMANDO CARLOS STIEFEL, THIRD CHILD OF MARIA
GANDOLLA DE STIEFEL AND CARLOS HENRY STIEFEL

PHOTO 19 - OFELIA, JUANA, ORMANDO, RITA, OTTO, OSCAR. SEATING: ABUELA MARÍA AND
ABUELO CARLOS WITH CHINGO. KIDS: TERE, YIYI, RAÚL, BETTY, CARLOS, JORGE, ENRIQUE,
AND LITA

26

PHOTO 21 - OSCAR WITH HIS FAVORITE HORSE

PHOTO 20 - FIRST
COMMUNION, COLEGIO DEL
SAGRADO CORAZON
JUNE 15, 1911

OSCAR
GUILLERMO
CRISTIAN, FIFTH
CHILD OF MARIA
G. DE STIEFEL AND
CARLOS H. STIEFEL

PHOTO 23 - OSCAR AND MARTA
JULY 1937

PHOTO 22 - MARINA AND
OSCAR, BOWIE, AZ

PHOTO 24 - OSCAR, PASCANAS, FUTBOL
TEAM

27

PHOTO 25 - INITIATION INTO JESUIT ORDER

OCTAVIO ARISTIDES
STIEFEL, SIXTH CHILD
OF MARIA G. DE STIEFEL
AND CARLOS H. STIEFEL

PHOTO 26 - OCTAVIO AND
OTTO, FIRST COMMUNION,
TEMPLO DEL S.S.
SACRAMENTO,
MARCH 12, 1914

PHOTO 27 - OCTAVIO,
EDITH, AND FRIENDS

OTTO MARIO
STIEFEL, SEVENTH
AND YOUNGEST
CHILD OF MARIA G.
DE STIEFEL AND
CARLOS H. STIEFEL

PHOTO 28 - OFELIA, OSCAR,
OCTAVIO, AND OTTO

TOP ROW, LEFT TO
RIGHT: SARA,
UNKNOWN, DORA,
PIRO, PIRA, MARIA,
AND DUILIO.
BOTTOM ROW,
FROM LEFT TO
RIGHT: RICARDO,
ULRICO, CARLOS H.,
OSCAR, AND OTTO
WITH LITTLE DOG.
PHOTO TAKEN IN
RIO CUARTO,
CÓRDOBA.

29

THE PEREGOS FROM CHIAVENNA, ITALY

GIOVANNI PEREGO'S HOUSE. INSIDE THE HOUSE, MAYA, SUCHI, DON GIOVANNI, NASTASSIA, AND MARTA PEREGO, GIOVANNI'S DAUGHTER.

DON GIOVANNI AND MARTA LOOKING A THE CHIODERA FAMILY SHIELD.

THE PEREGOS WITH FAMILY AND FRIENDS ENJOYING A PICNIC AT THEIR MOUNTAIN CABIN IN THE SMALL TOWN OF STAMPA, CLOSE TO THE SWITZERLAND BORDER

A PICTURE OF THE CABIN AND THE TRADITIONAL GRILL MADE FROM SHALE. THEY ALSO MAKE ASADITOS IN CHIAVENNA!

The traditional Torta di Fioretto

31

THE ARIATTA FAMILY IN MILANO: OLYMPIA AUREGGI ARIATTA, FRANCESCO ARIATTA, MARGHERITA ARIATTA AND CHILDREN, OLYMPIA AND FRANCESCO

HOUSE IN MILANO

PHOTO 30 - TERESINA PEREGO

PHOTO 29 - AMALIA PEREGO, 1865

PHOTO 31 - JOSÉ PEREGO (GIUSEPPE), BROTHER TO CATERINA AND AMALIA

PHOTO 32 - DUILIO PEREGO, SON OF GIOVANNI PEREGO AND OLIMPIA RIVA, AND HIS WIFE RITA MORO

PHOTO 33 – FUNERAL OF GIOVANNI PEREGO, HUSBAND OF OLIMPIA RIVA, 1914

DON GIOVANNI PEREGO AND OLIMPIA RIVA PEREGO, PARENTS OF GIOVANNI PEREGO. SHIELD IN CHIAVENNA IN HIS HONOR.

DIPLOMA GIVEN TO GIOVANNI PEREGO IN ROSARIO ON MARCH 31, 1878, FOR BEING A FOUNDING MEMBER OF THE SOCIEDAD ITALIANA DE UNION Y BENEVOLENCIA

ROSARIO, SOCIEDAD DE SOCORROS MUTUOS, FOUNDED BY GIOVANNI PEREGO IN 1861, CARLOS H. STIEFEL, STANDING, 5TH FROM LEFT. ARTURO GIARDINIERI, TO HIS RIGHT, SITTING. PLAQUE READS GUISEPPE MANZZINI, PATRIA- LAVORO

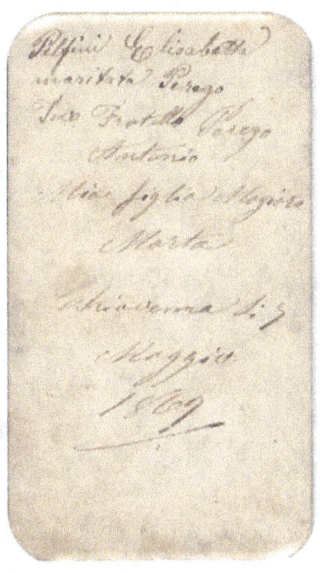

BACK OF PHOTO,
SENT FROM
ANTONIO TO HIS
SISTER, CATERINA

CATERINA PEREGO,
DAUGHTER OF
GIOVANNI PEREGO
AND OLIMPIA RIVA

ANTONIO PEREGO, HIS
WIFE ELIZABETTA PELFINI
PEREGO, AND DAUGHTER
MARTA PEREGO, 1989

GIULIA AND EUGENIA
CARUGATI, DAUGHTERS OF
CARLOTA PEREGO

CARLOTTA PEREGO,
DAUGHTER OF GIOVANNI
PEREGO AND OLIMPIA RIVA,
MARRIED TO LUIGI
CARUGATI

ANOTHER
PHOTO OF
EUGENIA
CARUGATI

DUILIO PEREGO, SON OF
GIOVANNI PEREGO AND
OLIMPIA RIVA

MARGHERITA PEREGO,
DAUGHTER OF GIOVANNI
PEREGO AND OLIMPIA RIVA

GIULIA RIVA, SISTER TO
OLIMPIA RIVA

ANOTHER PHOTO OF GIOVANNI PEREGO,
HUSBAND TO OLIMPIA RIVA

36

HOURGLASS TREE OF CHIODERA-PEREGO FAMILY

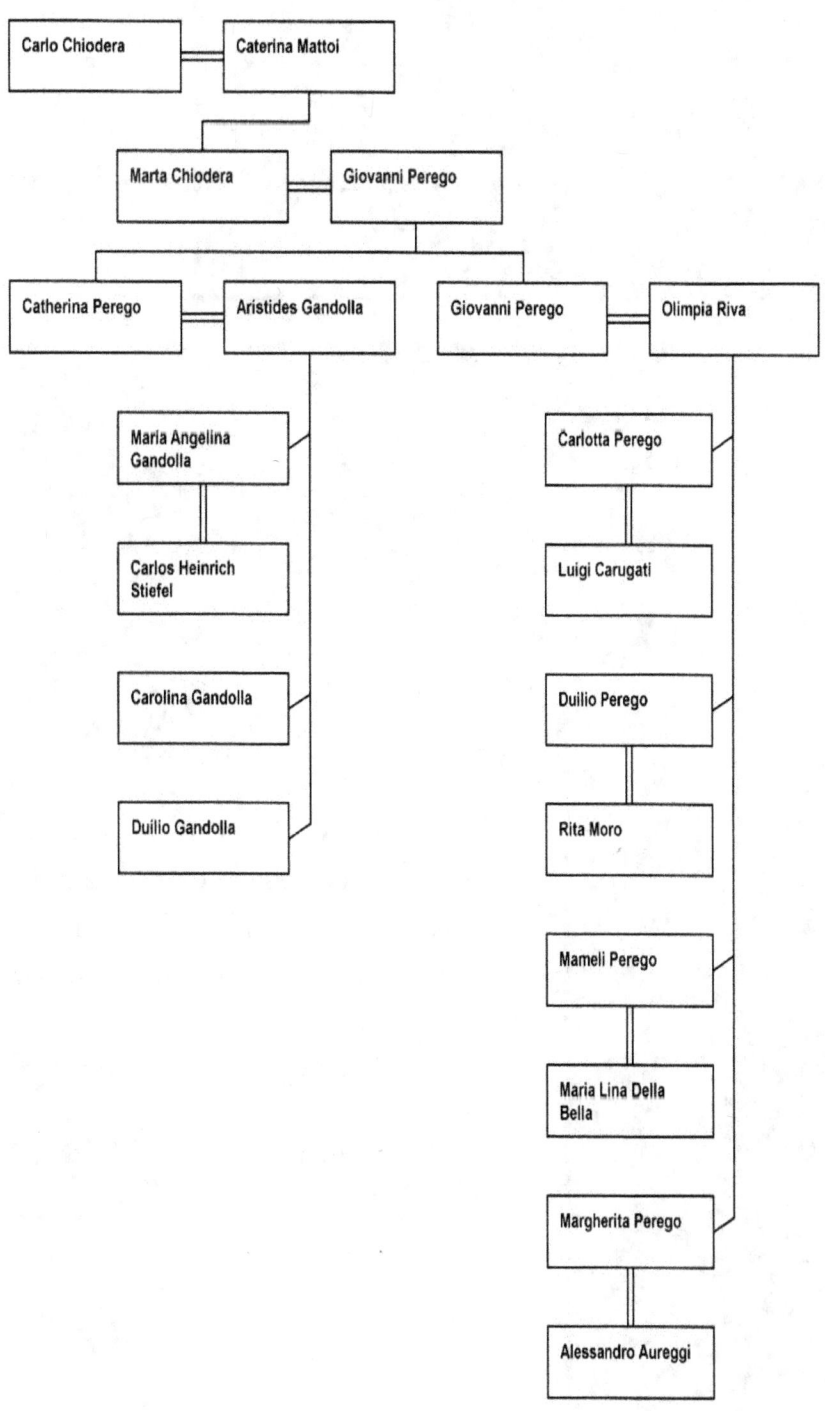

THE JEWERLY STORE THAT GIOVANNI PEREGO OWNED IN ROSARIO, CALLE PUERTO NO.141

According to Don Giovanni Perego, this picture corresponds to a carnival in Rosario, Santa Fé. The man in the costume is a family member.

"SOCIETA CARNAVALESCA CAMPIDOGLIO" STAMPED BEHIND THE IMAGE

SFORZESCO CASTLE IN MILANO

Sforzesco Castle is one of the most prominent symbols of Milano. Its construction began in the second half of the fourteenth century and it lasted until the beginning of the twentieth century, through different stages and difficulties.

Throughout its history, the Castle was intended for different uses: it started a garrison and then became the splendid residence of the Dukes of Milan, of the Visconti House at the beginning, and of the Sforza House at the end.

The castle flourished greatly throughout the Renaissance. The locals of Milano set out to rival the nobility that ruled in the rest of Italy and Europe who had been building their great palatial residences. As a result, the most outstanding artists of the time, such as Bramante and Leonardo, to name a few, arrived in Milan. During the rule of Ludovico Sforza, the Moor, Leonardo lived in the Castle; the sign of his genius is still admired in the celebrated Sala delle Asse.

After the final fall of the Lordship of Sforza, foreign dominations began: French and Spanish, earlier, and Austrian, later, until reaching the Cisalpine Republic. During this period, which was finished with the Unity of Italy, the Castle lost its aspect of princely palace and returned to its early function, that is, to house the garrison that was prominent during the Milanes Period.

In the late nineteenth century, the Castle became the property of the Milan City Council, and they began a wide campaign of rehabilitation and reconstruction to restore its old splendor and make it the seat of an important museum. This effort has continued until now and currently, several museums and collections are in the Castle. In its halls, there are works considered national and world artistic heritage, such as the famous Piedad Rondanini, Michelangelo's last masterpiece.

THE GANDOLLA-GRANT FAMILY FROM BELLAGIO

ANGELO GANDOLLA, ANGELA MARIA CURIONI, MARIA GANDOLLA CURIONI, PARENTS AND SISTERS OF ARISTIDES GANDOLLA. MISSING DOMENICO, ENRICO, AND ARISTIDES

PHOTO 34 - ARÍSTIDES GANDOLLA

CHILDREN OF MARGHERITA GRANT AND DOMENICO ENRICO GANDOLLA: EMMA, ENRICO, ARTURO, AND IDA

MARGHERITA GRANT, WIFE OF DOMENICO ENRICO GANDOLLA

41

PHOTO 35 - ARÍSTIDES GANDOLLA

PHOTO 36 - ARÍSTIDES AND
DOMENICO E. GANDOLLA

PHOTO 37 - ENRIQUE GANDOLLA SENN, JUAN
TISCORNIA, ARTURO GANDOLLA I/ECHAGUE, EMMA
GANDOLLA DE GIMENO, IDA GANDOLLA, MARGARITA
GRANT DE GANDOLLA, ZULEMA TISCORNIA DE
COPELLO

Hourglass Tree of Angelo Gandolla

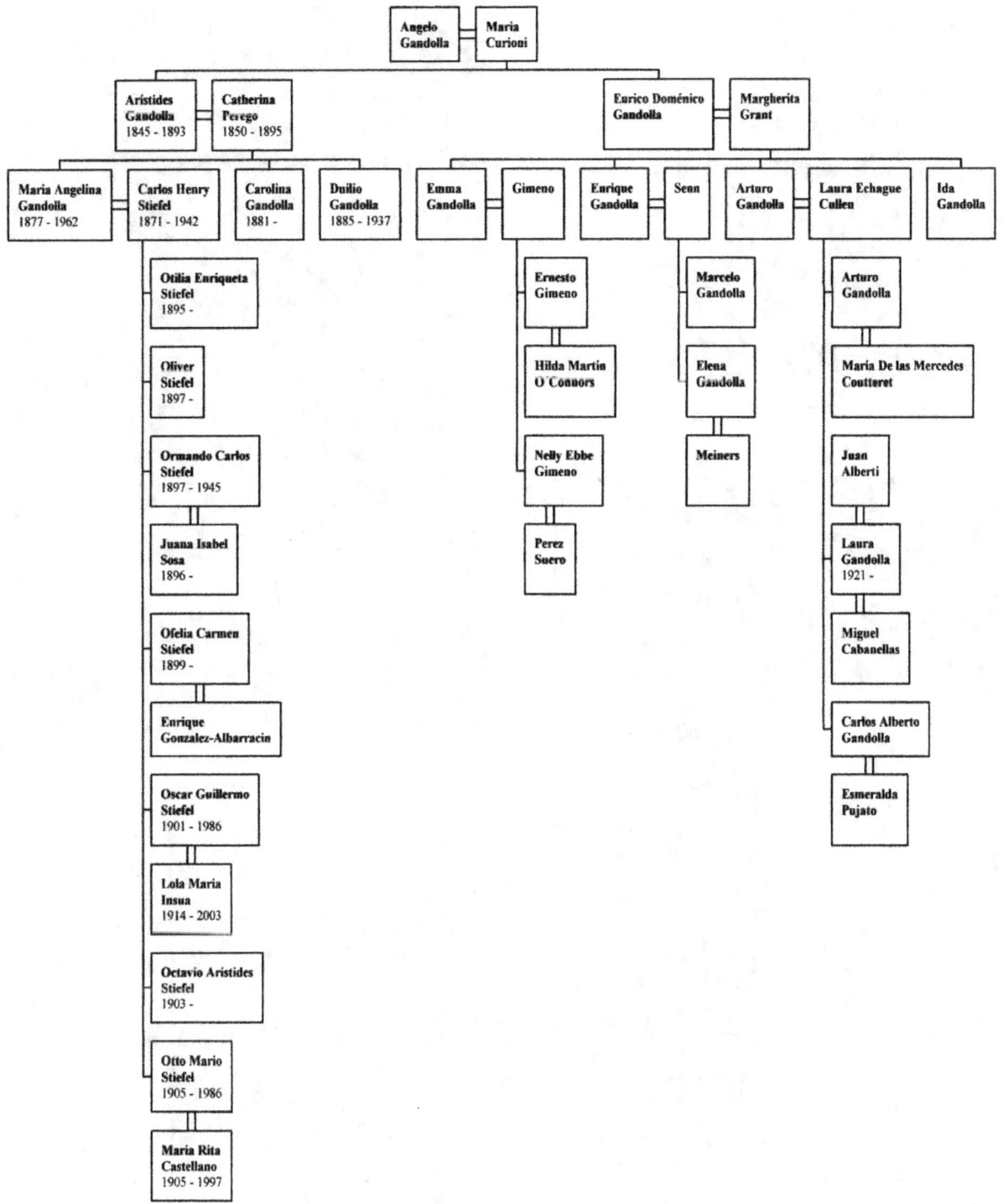

PHOTO 39 - ULRICO STIEFEL,
BROTHER OF CARLOS H. STIEFEL

PHOTO 38 - ABUELA MARÍA AND TÍA
CAROLINA, HER SISTER

PHOTO 40 - TERE AND RAÚL, CHILDREN
OF OTTO STIEFEL, FIRST COMMUNION,

ABUELA
MARÍA AND
ABUELO
CARLOS WITH
RAÚL, OTTO'S
SON

44

PHOTO 41 - JUANA WITH ISABEL, OSCAR, ABUELA MARÍA WITH RAÚL, ABUELO CARLOS, RITA AND OFELIA. CHILDREN: ENRIQUE, YIYI, LITA, JORGE, CARLITOS AND TERESITA.

PHOTO 42 - GALERÍA AT THE OLD HOUSE IN PASCANAS

LA ESTANCIA ALTO ALEGRE, PASCANAS

Padres de Carlos H. Stieff

1849   Berta Angelica Eschuy
       nació el 5 de Enero 1849.
       Büren Canton Solothurn (Suiza)
       Murió en Rosario de Sta Fé
1998   el dia 28 de Mayo 1998 —

       Carlos Guillermo Stieff.
1840.16 de Febrero nació en Forrnst
       Würtemberg (Alemania) 12 Dbre 1913

              — Hijos —

Agost 23 Carlos murió el 13 de Agosto
Oct   8   Emilia
Abr   27 Federico 1875
Oct   27 Ema murió en Sta Fé 20 de Enero 1928 —   187
Julio 4   Adela, murió 18 de Octubre 1914 en B Aires
Mayo   9   Ricardo
       9   Guillermo
       2   Mario

Carlos H. Stiefel.

1871 - 23 de Agosto, nació en Cañada de
San Geronimo - Pr. S.F.
Bautizado 19 de N.bre 1871 - en
la "Estancia Leones"
Testigos y Padrinos. Carlos Bauer - y Enrique
Usinger Murió el 1º de Agosto de 19
en Villa del Lago Cordoba -

1896 64 Confirmado el 14 de Marzo en la Iglesia de Pacua
por Monseñor Terrero - padrino Otto
Bauer en la Iglesia del Salvador. B. Aires por el
P. Roman

1936 Nuestros confirmados por Mon. Terrero en Pacua
Vera Stiefel, madrina M. Elena Stiefel
"   Lydia "   "   "   "   "
"   Luisa "   "   Maria G. de Stiefel
"   Manuela "   "   "   "
"   Beba   "   "   "   "
"   Elena   "   "   M. Rita C. de Stiefel
"   Carlitos "   Padrino Carlos H. Stiefel
"   Raul   "   "   Arturo Candelaria

48

Padres de Maria Angelina Gandolla Perez

Aristides Gandolla
nació en Bellaggio (Italia)
el 25 de Abril
Murió el 9 de Agosto 1893.
en Rosario de Sta Fé
se casó en Rosario a los 31 años - 16 de Agosto 1876
(Padres) Angel Gandolla - Maria Curione)

Catalina Perego
Nació el 25 de Abril en Chiavenna
Italia, casó el 6 de Agosto a los 26 años en Rosario de Sta Fé
Murió en Carlos Pellegrini
el 14 de Marzo 1895.
(Padres) Juan Perego y M Marta Chiroleu -

- Hijos -
1847 Maria Angelina nació el 23 de Junio
1881 Carolina   " " 26 de Agosto
1885 Amelia   " " 12 "   " murió 13 Junio 1937

Maria A. Gandolla Peres

1877-23 Nació en Rosario de Santa Fe el
23 de Junio de 1877. Bautizada en
Rosario. Madrina _____ Gandolla

La Primera Comunión en _____
en la Iglesia de las _____ el 25
de Junio 1890.

Casó el 16 de Nbre en _____
de 1901 y por _____ el 14 del mismo
mes en C. _____

Padrinos _____

Padrinos de bautismo _____ G de Gandolla
y Anibal _____ el 17 de Agosto de 1978 en Ros_____

The Borracho and the Virgen were at Abuela María's house in Villa del Lago.

The Virgen was inside a niche in the bedroom.

The Borracho was on top of a shelf in the dining room.

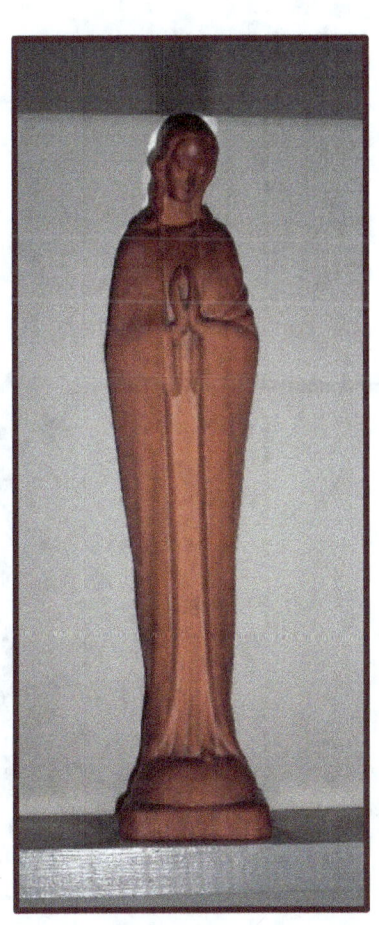

VILLA DEL LAGO, CÓRDOBA

PHOTO 43 - THE WHOLE FAMILY IN VILLA DEL LAGO, CIRCA 1947

PHOTO 44 - MARTA LAURA WITH ABUELA MARÍA
IN VILLA DEL LAGO, 1949

FAMILY STORIES
RECOUNTED
BY THE PROTAGONISTS,
WITHOUT SPARING
DETAILS AND WITHOUT
EXAGGERATING TOO
MUCH, THE WAY
THEY WERE TOLD
TO ME,
WITHOUT CHANGING
ANY PARTICULARS,
SO THAT NEW
GENERATIONS WOULD
KNOW HOW WE LIVED OUR
LIVES BACK THEN…

LOS CUENTOS DE TATANA/TATANA'S TALES

Río del Medio

El papi (Enrique González Albarracín) bought that property in 1934, without seeing the place, because of sweet memories from his childhood and sentimental reasons, since his mother was the very first teacher in the town of Los Reates. He bought those acres without knowing where they were. The property was called Chincaj Wayco, which in Quechua, means Quebrada Escondida, because it is located in a small valley, between two municipalities, Santa María and Calamuchita, and it is divided by the Río del Medio, so we fulfilled our dream of having our own river, since nobody went there, only our family and friends.

When my father bought that land, it only had a tiny adobe house with a wooden porch and a thatched roof, with dirt floors, like all the mountain houses then. He devoted himself to improve it, making new floors that were coated, and fixing them as needed throughout the years. That land was not good to raise any crops since it was all rocky, and it was only possible to grow corn in only two places; there was another place dedicated to a beautiful vegetable garden; those who saw the vegetable garden were amazed. In front, before reaching the house, we had to cross the river; he made a ford so we could cross it and get to the house. As he liked everything related to the countryside, he bought the magazine Revista La Chacra, and from there he learned and taught both his children, as well as the locals, to live better and improve their standard of living, not discriminating between their children, and us; we all had to work, according to our age, the older boys had to fix the barbed wire, the pircas (stone walls), and chopped the firewood.

The good water was put in an earthen jar to keep it cool for drinking. We went to the river, at 6 p.m. and collected the water in buckets. It was easy going but returning was hard because the buckets were very heavy, carrying the water and climbing to the house, which was about 3 blocks away. Behind the house ran a stream but that water was good for washing dishes and for general cleaning, nothing more.

Later, my father started buying animals; we had horses, cows, pigs, chickens, ducks, and I don't remember what else; we had every domesticated animal. Then, with the improvements, he made a small dam, upstream, to make an acequia. With the water that ran in the acequia, the vegetable garden was watered, and all kinds of vegetables and fruits were grown. There were 125 peach trees, and, in the summer, we would sit, under a willow, to peel the fruit to make jam. They were made in large quantities, for the whole family, and to give away. The Guindado liquor was the only one that mother made, for the winter; it was the only liquor that was consumed at home. There were also all kinds of jams and marmalades from peaches, apricots, grapes, quince, figs; we preserved the fruit in all forms, in jams and in syrup. In the vegetable garden, there was also a tobacco patch; the youngest, were the ones in charge of cutting the leaves, thread them with a needle and thread and put them to dry in a shed, then, after being dry, we chopped them, and we stored in jars, with slices of apples, so that the tobacco would stay humid; my father and my brothers and I learned to smoke home-made cigarettes.

I remember that with my brother Cheche, we went to the river to smoke, and then, before we came up to the house, we chewed mint or peperina leaves, so that we did not smell of cigarettes. With Cheche, who was only two years older than me, we did a lot of mischief, of all kinds; he was the one with the ideas and I was the companion in all of his shenanigans; I was his accomplice, and he manipulated me nicely.

Very close to the house we had a hill, and at its top there was a thorn bush (Espinillo). According to Cheche, at the base of the bush, there was a gold mine. So, at nap time, we both would go, hidden from mother, carrying a shovel and pickaxe. I do not remember seeing any snakes, but I imagine that there were many, but they never bother us. It was very hard to carry the shovel and pickaxe for me because they were very heavy, but hey, I did it. One day, Yiyi, my oldest sister, who was dating Manolo, was given some golden earrings; Cheche took them, broke them and when we got down from what he said was his gold mine, but which had only mica, (big difference), he showed the broken hoops, and Yiyi realized that they were hers, and almost killed us both.

Another year, Susy, our cousin, went with us to spend the summer vacation. Our house was being remodeled, and at this moment, we were, mother, Susy, Teresita, Chingo and I; we would have been, me 10 years old, Susy 12, and Teresita 5. Chingo, was not at the house at that time, since he had gone to Roca's house, because this lady was making a portrait of him. Their house was far away, so he went on horseback, and on his return trip a great storm came, which caught him in the middle of a field. We were in one room far from the house, and in the afternoon the storm came, with rain and hail, which lasted 30 minutes; the hail was small, but it destroyed all the plants on the vegetable garden. I was crying, mom was lighting blessed palms and candles. All three of us were very scared. Teresita was sleeping, and mom told me not to cry, so as not to wake her up; it was raining down on us. In the morning when we got up, we found everything as if it were wintertime, bare trees, dead birds, and we went to the cow's corral, and we found only one heifer, of the five that were there the day before. The hail was 1.50 meters high; we got scared thinking they would be under the accumulated hail, but no, they had escaped, just like the cows.

I remember that we had only one match, and we had to light the wood fire for cooking, so, we lit a candle, with that single match, in order to preserve the fire. Mom was worried, thinking about Chingo, hoping nothing had happened to him. She sent us to the river, to see if he was coming. The river was growing, and we were taking turns to tell him not to cross it, to stay in the house at the front, until the river went down, but he was worried, not for us, but for a horse that he had, and while we were up, he crossed it, because it was his habit of crossing the river when it was swollen. Poor mother with all her problems, with her 8 children and her illness. Between the dining room and the kitchen, there was a deep pantry, with two doors facing each other. There, my horse got stuck inside; we didn't know how to get him out, as the pantry was narrow and long. It took a lot of work to get the horse out of there, but he came out finally. In addition, we had another room, outside the house, which was another pantry, where there was a cooler room, where we put the vegetables and meat to preserve it, it had no glass windows, only metallic fabric, and there we kept the bags of flour, yerba mate, sugar, and other things that were brought wholesale.

The previous weekend, father had brought us three large cans of cookies, but water got inside the cans, and they all got wet, we were so sad. I think Susy isn't going to forget this summer ever.

Again, mother sent Teresita and me to Los Reartes, on horseback, to take some fruit to some relatives who spent the summer there; we carried the peaches in some saddlebags, loose, and went galloping when we could. When we got there and gave them the peaches, they looked like a smoothy, due to the bumping of the saddlebags against the belly of the horse, it was a disaster.

We spent the most beautiful summers in that place, we had freedom, we would eat fruit, we would ride horses, ride in a sulky or in a cart, we would bathe in the river, and we would read, we would listen to music with a victrola, which we had to crank with the handle. I remember this summer with Susy, the victrola did not work, the crank handle had been broken, so we turned the with our finger, and another person held the membrane, I think that is the name; and as the needle was worn, we used black acacia spines, and we only had one record, which was called "You have bought a car", and that record played all day.

Another anecdote of Rio del Medio.

Since I was born, the last vertebrae of my spinal column are welded, and is congenital, so I do not have a good mobility and have problems with my column. When I wanted to ride a horse, I couldn't jump on top of the horse, as everyone else did, I had to look for a big stone, a chair or anything, to step on it. On one of the trips to The Reartes, the saddle cinch got loose, and we were just in the middle of an open field, where there was not a large stone to stand and be able to get on the horse, after adjusting the cinch, I had to look for a stone to be able to step on, but there was none. It was difficult, but I succeeded.

Those summers bring me so many beautiful memories when I went to Río del Medio. Going there was a whole odyssey at that time, with very old cars, from the 40s. We left in the early morning, mom, dad, Cheche and Teresita. We had breakfast at the Alta Gracia Crossroads, it was coffee with milk, in very large white stone cups, with the milk foam on top, then we continued traveling and in La Serranita, we made another stop, where we ate a sandwich with that farm bread, the crust was hard, and the inside was too. This was a very special bread, which in olden times was everywhere, but we can no longer find it. We arrived at the house after 5 hours of traveling, when the road was good, and we encounter no rain. Otherwise, we needed to use those famous chains on the car wheels, so as not to get stuck. At that time, there was no Dique los Molinos. At the present time, this trip can be done in an hour and a half. On one of the trips, we got stuck in the mud, and after a while, some locals appear, carrying a wooden coffin with a dead person inside; they were going to bury him in Los Reartes, but when they saw us, they left the coffin on the side of the road and helped us out of the swamp where we were.

Another time, the three youngest ones were with our mom at home, when the Justice of the Peace, who lived near our home, about a kilometer away, came to ask mom, if we could hold the prisoners in any of the rooms of the house, since he had no place to put them and held them tied to a tree. Of course, mom said no, since at the time, there were none of my male siblings in the house. So many things have happened to us there, both good and bad. When my mom was sick, with her cancer, at a time mommy was unwell, dad left us a car and the driver, in case something happened to her. That driver was called Anacleto Oliva, and he loved my mom very much. At that time, we still had the first rancho and Oliva slept in a cot, in the porch, next to the door of mom's bedroom, just in case something happened to her, so he could help her right away, and so he did every night, until the last week, when dad came back from Córdoba.

I preferred to spend my summers here, at Río del Medio, instead of Villa del Lago, at the house of Abuela María. Here we had more fun, more freedom, it was something different. Here we lacked everything, electricity, refrigerator, running water, things that were available at the grandmother's house. That house had all the comforts, but we preferred this country life, where we learned to do everything, to milk the cows and drink the milk at the cow's feet, to have breakfast with the homemade bread, with the jam and butter made by us. In the middle of the morning, we loved to yogurt or the mazamorra with milk, the big lunches, with all homemade ingredients, in the afternoon the tea and mate with pastries, and in the evening the same the great food. I will not forget the yemitas, which mom made with a fresh egg yolk, and 5 tablespoons of sugar; we beat the mixture very well, with a fork, until the sugar was dissolved and was all fluffy. Mom added Marsala or Port to hers; or the soft-boiled eggs, with a running yolk, mixed with breadcrumbs, how delicious!

There are many memories, as we washed our clothes in the river and the wool from mattresses that we washed also in the river. How much wool and how many clothes the river took when we got careless. Another tradition was to wash the cars in the river, using buckets. We loved to do that! and to think that on the trip back to Córdoba, the cars again were filled with dirt, really, I don't know why we did it, but it was fun, because while washing the car, we splattered water on each other.

When someone was coming by car to visit us, I loved to wait and see how they try to go through the ford and make the climb to the house. Sometimes, they could not, and the car got turned around on the ford and if they did not know how to drive very well, they would fall into the river. Chingo told them how they had to do it so that the car did not stop and slide down back to the river. This is how I learned how to cross the ford since there was a very steep climb through stones just after the ford.

 It was also fascinating to watch the storms, the lightning, and how the sky lit up and on starry nights, watching the sky, it was wonderful, as it was all dark, there were no lights anywhere and the stars looked much brighter. We gathered the tucos (lightening bugs) in a jar; they have hard shells, at least one centimeter long, with wings, and have the light always on, not like the fireflies.

I learned so much during those summers, about the countryside, its customs, its foods, the local tales, to ride a horse, to swim and so many things. We learned to watch how the animals react to rain, how they announce it. We learned that if it rained in Cumbrecita, where the river is born, you'll have the rising in five hours, listening to the sound when it approaches, which sounds like thunder or a car or an airplane. Dad made 3 suspension bridges, so that he could cross the river, but the risings took them away. We saw the stream increase and take many trees, such as wicker trees and willows. Really, all this I carry in my blood and in my memory because I have lived among the mountains, I am used to them, bathing in rivers of transparent waters, seeing the bottom, their stones. The sea I do not like, I get dizzy with the waves, and I am afraid of that immensity, and it is the same with the plains; it is like feeling helpless. Instead, the mountains contained me, I feel sheltered, I do not know why, but it is what I feel, that is why I like so much the place where I live, as I tell my children, I feel like a tree, with its roots here and in this climate, if they take them out, they die. Only those of us who have lived here, know it and it feels like a part of oneself.

Villa del Lago

Villa del Lago, we named it Heaven and Hell, because of our grandmother, who made us work and cook, did not let us bathe in the lake, or leave the property, out of fear. Abuela Maria would wake us up at 6 in the morning, put the radio on very loud to wake us up, then we would go to her room. She drank her mate and we would sit on her bed around her; she would tell us stories, made up by her, but always with some teaching, then everyone had their tasks: mostly cleaning the house, but she made Susy and I cook. The meals we made! Once I had to make potato gnocchi, and I served them, they were all sticky, they were horrible, but we had to eat them anyway, since she said, that in the war, many people would have wish to eat that dish and we wanted to waste it. We made lunch at 11 am, also we had to take a nap and she went to bed at 7 pm and would close the whole house and we had to go to bed, but we, who were accustomed to going to bed at 9 or 10 pm thought it was too early. There were also the rosaries; we prayed on the rotunda at 5 pm and we saw our friends passing by on a sailboat and we were there praying. There were many incidents like these ones and when we meet with Susy and Mimi, we remembered those so-called vacations. One thing, we read a lot, especially grandmother's books, she was an avid reader, books by Pérez and Pérez, she had the complete collection, plus the magazine El ParaTí, which she collected.

I also remember a vacation in San Javier and another trip to San Clemente, with mom, Gorgo, Tía Otilia, Ernesto and I, in our father's car, which he lent us, and we went to visit Octavio who was there, and our car broke down, and Octavio had to take us and bring us back by truck, at night. Poor Tía Otilia arrived at the convent at about 3 in the morning.

Pascanas and Familia

I don't want to say anything about Pascanas. I never lived there, because when my parents returned from Europe, they stayed in Córdoba, because mom was already sick from cancer the tongue, so that's why we did not go back Pascanas. I saw my parents' house, when I went on a trip to Wenceslao Escalante for work, and I drove through Pascanas, and so I saw the house and our grandfather's business, but I never went back again, I know only everything that I heard and was told. Dad, Enrique Jacinto González-Albarracín was the first mayor of Pascanas, and they paid tribute to him. They have a picture of him in the Quartermaster's Office. I could not go to the ceremony. My father's mother was called Restituta Albarracín de González, but as González was a very common surname, to differentiate it the two names were hyphenated together. I don't think anyone knows the real name of my brothers and sisters; they are only known by their nicknames:

Lita - Ofelia Nélida
Yiyi - Elvia Ester
Pelado - Enrique Alberto
Gorgo - Jorge Raúl
Chingo - Carlos Iván
Cheche - Omar Emilio
Tatana - Susana del Carmen
Teresita - Mirta Teresita

El LINYERA (The Wanderer)

TATANA Thursday, April 29, 2010, 7:07 PM
"SUSANA GONZALEZ ALBARRACIN" <tatana1936@gmail.com>
"Marta Stiefel Ayala, Ph.D." <periquita88@yahoo.com>

Marta, our famous uncle, "the Linyera," I think his name was Eustaquio, I believed he lived in Despeñaderos, but there is another version, according to Oscar, who said he was a German. I don't know if he was our great-grandfather's brother. He was a great professor, and during vacations, he traveled all over Europe and Argentina, it was said, riding the trains without paying. He was like a linyera (wanderer), and he carried a backpack full of books, and had a lot of stories to tell. He came unannounced, stayed a few days and left abruptly without telling anyone. Everybody was very deferential to him and was offered the best seat at the table. Supposedly, he was a great scholar, and when classes were about to start, he went home, he bathed, he groomed himself very well, and he went to teach his classes, crazy, right?
I just talked to Elena, to ask her about him, she also knows the story, but not as I thought; she said he was not from Despeñaderos, but from Pascana, yes, she knows that his name was Eustaquio, but she does not know anything about the kinship.
I just talked to Susy; she also remembers our grandmother's story. It seems that he was from Pascanas, and I started to look for the relationship he had with our grandfather, he must have been a cousin, since I did not find any Eustaquios as Grandpa Carlos' brother. Who knows what relationship the grandfather had with this madman? We will find out, do not worry, but the story is true.
A kiss to the two of you.
Tatana

PHOTOS OF RIO DEL MEDIO SHOWING HOUSE AND RIVER AS DESCRIBED BY
TATANA ON HER TALES

More photos on page 100

LETTERS FROM ITALY

Milano,13 gennaio 1988

Estimado Arquitecto
Onias Ernesto Carreño
Calle Mitre IO
0324 CIPOLLETTI
Rio Negro =Rep.Argentina

Carissimi Susanna ed Ernesto,

abbiamo ricevuto con molto gradimento la Vostra

carissima lettera e la partecipazione del casamiento di Alejandro e Inés Maria:

MUCHAS FELICIDADES!   Un grande abbraccio a tutti! Partecipamos a Vuestra fiesta

Noi ritardiamo a rispondere perchè Francesco è stato un po' all'estero per trabajo

e inoltre perchè volevamo parlarvi delle cassettas che in albergo NON hanno più trova

#anno detto che sicuramente sono state rubate da obreros che hacen limpieza.

De toda manera muchas gracias!

Hablamos sempre di Voi con Giovanni e Emma   e Vi ricordiamo sempre con tanto piacere

tutti Voi cari parenti.Marta Perego   di Giovanni   non ha potuto incontrare

Marta Stiefel in San Diego perchè perchè falta la direccion:Uds pueden enviarla a n

sotros? Non abbiamo visto Ignacio della Democrazia Cristiana,pensavamo di vederlo

durante la visita del Presidente Alfonsin in Italia.

La torta di fioretto è: pasta da pane (pasta de pan) con uova (6 per I KG di

farina) e burro (manteca : 300 hg /350 per I Kg di farina) e sopra un impasto di

zucchero, manteca e fiore di finocchio (hinoco), tutto cotto al forno.   Fateci

sapere se è chiara la receta de la torta? Se no, la invio più chiara.Ditemi

se siete riusciti a realizzarla.

Con muchos gusto attendemos las fotos del casamiento per conoscere tutta la famiglia.

Con piacere Vi invieremo foto e cartoline di Chiavenna e di Bellagio.

Bellagio è il paese del Vostro bisnonno Gandola (marito di Caterina Perego).

E' un paese molto molto bello e Vi manderemo le cartoline. Un parente di Vs.

61

di Voi con la mia mamma; ma temo che siano morti perchè erano molto viejos.
Mi informerò dei loro figli.= Sono sempre state gente muchias distinguidas.
Quando la Vostra abuela Mria è venuta in Italia volevamo condurla a trovare
il sig.Pietro Gandola a Lecco e poi a Bellagio a vedere il paese, ma= lastima
que se quedó poco tiempo! Così la abuela non ha potuto incotrare il sig.
Gandola.
Il giorno di Natale Vi abbiamo pensati tutti uniti, anche   con Alejandro e Inés:
BUON ANNO! MUCHAS FELICIDADES!
Muchias gracias per la invitacion in Argentina,sarebbe proprio bello conoscere
tutta la Vostra cara famiglia, ma per ora non è possibile venire,ma ci rivedremo
in Italia. Ora Margherita studia molto per laurearsi in derecho nella
Università Cattolica di Milano, speriamo che finisca ntro il 1989 , se todo
sigue bien. Marta è arrivata a Chiavenna da San Diego per Natale, ma è già
ripartita per tornare a San Diego. Anche con Marta abbiamo parlato molto
di Voi e hemos tomado una copa a la salud de Susana, Ernesto y todas la
familia   dei parenti argentini.
Qui è freddo,   siamo in inverno, però non nevica per grazia di Dio.Noi andiamo
sempre tutte le domeniche a Chiavenna per la mia attività di avvocato.
Aspettiamo la primavera per coltivare anche noi i fiori nel nostro giardino
e mettere in funzione la vasca nel centro del giardino. Vi penseremo ;peccato
essere così lontani: potremmo scambiarci le qualità di fiori.
Con molta probabilità nel verano andremo a fare una crociera con la=
il barco Eugenio C. (lina Costa, che viene anche in Argentina): noi NON
arriveremo in Argentina, ma andremo in Spagna, Marocco, Canarie, Madeira,
Azzorre, Portogallo. Il barco è bello e con molto divertimento; uesta è
l'unica occasione che teniamo per descansar,perchè tutto l'anno siamo
sempre molto occupati. Vi manderemo cartoline della crociera.

Un grande abbraccio, beso cariño aff. Olimpia, Margherita
Marta junto *Francesco*
62

Re: hello
Monday, October 12, 2009, 3:08 PM
From: Ariatta" <arìatta@email.it>
To: "Dr. Reynaldo Ayala" nanasbooks@yahoo.com

Carissima Marta,
chiedo scusa per il ritardo nel rispondere a Voi ed a Susanna e anche nell'identificare alcune fotografie: abbiamo avuto tanto lavoro per la nostra professione. Sui Chiodera Dalla Chiesa posso assicurarTi che si trattava di una famiglia importante e distinta: discendevano dalla famiglia Mascaranico, i cui membri erano banchieri e discendevano anche da un ramo della famiglia Rusca che era signora di Como nel 1400. Giovan Battista Dalla Chiesa aveva solo la figlia Marta che aveva sposato Filippo Chiodera di Gravedona, sul lago di Como, appartenente a una famiglia importante, figlio di ser Giuseppe. A Chiavenna c'era la famiglia Mattoi, tirolese, di origine di Pfunz, in Austria, al confine con la Svizzera. Paolo Antonio Mattoi, vedovo con una bambina, Caterina, si è risposato con Marta Chiodera, figlia di Filippo e di Marta Dalla Chiesa; Marta Chiodera Mattoi si è tanto affezionata allá figlia del marito e l'ha fatta sposare al proprio fratello Carlo Chiodera: da questi due sposi è nata Marta Chiodera, moglie di Giovanni Perego senior e madre di Giovanni Perego Junior, marito di Olympia Riva, ed è nata anche Caterina, sposata Gandola. Da Marta Mattoi Chiodera sono nati due maschi, Filippo e Giacomo, molto colti e intraprendenti: Filippo era molto ricco, portava degli enorme baffi ed era nonno di Olympia Riva, moglie di Giovanni Perego (Olympia Riva e Giovanni Perego erano parenti tra loro). Giacomo è morto molto prima di Filippo, lasciando la moglie Giulia Torricella De Balbiani, ultima discendente dei conti di Chiavenna, e tre bambine. Fatemi sapere se Vi interessano altre notizie. Un caro saluto, Olympia e Margherita

Re: hello
Monday, October 12, 2009 3:08 PM
From: Ariatta" <arìatta@email.it>
To: "Dr. Reynaldo Ayala" nanasbooks@yahoo.com

Dearest Marta, I apologize for the delay in responding to you and Susana and in the identification of some photos: we have had so much work in our profession. Related to the Chiodera Dalla Chiesa, I can assure you that it was an important and distinguished family; they descended from the Mascaranico family, whose members were bankers and also descended from a branch of the Rusca family who were lords of Como in 1400. Giovani Battista Dalla Chiesa had only one daughter Marta who had married Filippo Chiodera from Gravedona, on Lake Como, belonging to an important family, son of Giuseppe. In Chiavenna there was the Mattoi family, tyrolean, originating in Pfunz, in Austria, on the border with Switzerland. Paolo Antonio Mattoi, a widower with a little girl, Caterina, married to Marta Chiodera, daughter of Filippo and Marta Dalla Chiesa; Marta Chiodera Mattoi became so fond of her husband's daughter that she made her

64

marry her brother Carlo Chiodera: from this marriage was born Marta Chiodera, wife of Giovanni Perego senior and mother of Giovanni Perego Junior, husband of Olympia Riva, and Caterina was also born, who married Gandolla. From Marta Mattoi Chiodera were born two males, Filippo and Giacomo, very educated and enterprising: Filippo was very rich, with a big mustache, and was the grandfather of Olimpia Riva, wife of Giovanni Perego (Olimpia Riva and Giovanni Perego were relatives to each other). Giacomo died long before Filippo, leaving his wife Giulia Torricella De Balbiani, the last descendant of the counts of Chiavenna, and three children. Let me know if you are interested in other news.

A warm greeting, Olympia and Margherita

Re: hello
Wednesday, October 21, 2009 2:23 PM
From: "Ariatta" <ariatta@email.it>
To: Dr. Reynaldo Ayala" <nanasbooks@yahoo.com>

Carissima Marta,
non abbiamo piú i ritratti dipinti a olio di Filippo Chiodera, Marta Dalla Chiesa, Giovan Battista Chiodera: sono bruciati quando la nostra casa di Chiavenna è stata in parte devastata da un incendio nel 1914. Mia mamma mi diceva che nei ritratti tutti avevano la parrucca bianca, tipica del '700. Giovanni Perego senior e Marta Chiodera, oltre alle tre gemelle, tra cui Caterina, hanno avuto Giovanni Junior, marito di Olympia Riva, Giuseppe, morto in Argentina senza figli, Antonio, marito di Elisabetta Pelfini, che ha avuto un figlio maschio emigrato in America, una figlia femmina sposata a Berlino e un'altra figlia, Erina, che è morta a Chiavenna, non sposata, nel 1939, molto buona e brava; due bambine, figlie di Antonio ed Elisabetta Pelfini sono morte piccole, di una, Marta, abbiamo il ritratto. Giovanni Perego junior aveva anche una sorella, Maria, sposata a un avvocato Della Vita, a loro unica figlia non si è sposata ed è morta da tempo. Altri fratellini e sorelline di Giovannijunior sono morti piccoli. Antonietta era Antonietta Carugati, figlia di Carlotta Perego, sposata con l'avvocato Varcaponti, è morta senza figli; tutti i figli di Carlotta Perego sono morti senza figli, tranne Giovanni, che ha avuto una sola figlia, che vive a Milano: io l'ho invitata ad unirsi a noi quando Voi siete venute, mai suoi impegni di lavoro glielo hanno impedito (è ragioniera in una grande ditta, ha un figlio di 15 anni). Un'altra Antonietta era la figlia di Teresa Rizzi, che si è incontrata con la vostra avuela, quando è venuta nel 1950; Antonietta, figlia di Teresa, era la marnma di Mariuccia Comotti, di cui Vi ho già scritto, e nonna di Giulia Cassina, che abita a Londra. Sto guardando le fotografie e Vi risponderò a breve. Non so nulla dei Gandola, tranne che erano di Bellagio, della frazione di Pescallo.
Un abbraccio. A presto

Carissima Marta, we no longer have the oil-painted portraits of Filippo Chiodera, Marta Dalla Chiesa, Giovani Battista Chiodera: they burned when our house in Chiavenna was partly devastated by a fire in 1914. My mother told me that in the portraits everyone had the white wig, typical of the '700. Giovanni Perego senior and Marta Chiodera, in addition to the three twins, including Caterina, had Giovanni Junior, husband of Olympia Riva, Giuseppe, who died in Argentina without children, Antonio, husband of Elisabetta Pelfini, who had a male son who emigrated to America, a daughter married in Berlin and another daughter, Erina, who died in Chiavenna, unmarried, in 1939, very good and able; two girls, daughters of Antonio and Elisabetta Pelfini died small, of one, Marta, we have her portrait. Giovanni Perego junior also had a sister, Maria, married to a lawyer Della Vita, their only dauther, I do not know if she married and died a long time ago. Other little brothers and sisters of Giovanni junior died young. Antonietta was Antonietta Carugati, daughter of Carlotta Perego, married to the lawyer Varcaponti, died without children; all of Carlotta Perego's children died without children, except Giovanni, who had only one daughter, who lives in Milan. I had invited her to join us when you came, but her work commitments prevented her (she is an accountant in a large company, she has a 15-year-old son). The other one, Antoinetta was the daughter of Teresa Rizzi, who met with your grandmother María when she arrived in 1950; Antonietta, Teresa's daughter, was the mother of Mariuccia Comotti, of whom I have already written to you, and grandmother of Giulia Cassina, who now lives in London. I am looking at the photos and I will answer you shortly. I do not know anything about the Gandollas, except that they were from Bellagio, from the hamlet of Pescallo. A hug. Later. Olympia with Margherita

MARTA CHIODERA'S DEATH CERTIFICATE

DESCENDANTS OF CARLO CHIODERA

Generation 1

CARLO CHIODERA. He married CATERINA MATTOI.

Carlo Chiodera and Caterina Mattoi had the following child:

i.   MARTA CHIODERA was born in 1810 in Chiavenna, Sondrio, Lombardia, Italy. She died in 1886 in Chiavenna, Sondrio, Lombardia, Italy. She married GIOVANNI PEREGO. He was born in 1808. He died on 16 Dec 1863 in Milano, Lombardia, Italy.

Generation 2

MARTA CHIODERA was born in 1810 in Chiavenna, Sondrio, Lombardia, Italy. She died in 1886 in Chiavenna, Sondrio, Lombardia, Italy. She married GIOVANNI PEREGO. He was born in 1808. He died on 16 Dec 1863 in Milano, Lombardia, Italy.

Giovanni Perego and Marta Chiodera had the following children:

i.   CATHERINA PEREGO was born on 25 Apr 1850 in Chiavenna, Sondrio, Lombardia, Italy. She died on 14 Mar 1895 in Carlos Pellegrini, Santa Fé, Argentina. She married ARÍSTIDES GANDOLLA, son of Angelo Gandolla and Angela Maria Curioni on 06 Aug 1876.He was born on 25 Apr 1845 in Bellagio, Italy. He died on 09 Aug 1893 in Rosario, Santa Fé, Argentina.

ii.   GIOVANNI PEREGO was born in 1835. He died on 16 Dec 1914 in Chiavenna, Sondrio, Lombardia, Italy. He married OLIMPIA RIVA.

Generation 3

CATHERINA PEREGO (Marta Chiodera, Carlo Chiodera) was born on 25 Apr 1850 in Chiavenna, Sondrio, Lombardia, Italy. She died on 14 Mar 1895 in Carlos Pellegrini, Santa Fé, Argentina. She married ARÍSTIDES GANDOLLA, son of Angelo Gandolla and Angela Maria Curioni on 06 Aug 1876. He was born on 25 Apr 1845 in Bellagio, Italy. He died on 09 Aug 1893 in Rosario, Santa Fé, Argentina.

Arístides Gandolla and Catherina Perego had the following children:

i.   MARÍA ANGELINA GANDOLLA was born on 23 Jun 1877 in Rosario, Santa Fé, Argentina. She died on 25 Jul 1962 in Córdoba, Argentina. She married CARLOS H. STIEFEL Nov 1894 in Carlos Pellegrini, Santa Fé, Argentina. He was born on 23 Aug 1871 in Cañada del Arbol, Dept. San Gerónimo, Santa Fé, Argentina. He died on 01 Aug 1942 in Villa del Lago, Córdoba, Argentina.

ii.   CAROLINA GANDOLLA was born on 26 Aug 1881 in Rosario, Santa Fé, Argentina. Not married.

iii.   DUILIO GANDOLLA was born on 12 Aug 1885 in Rosario, Santa Fé, Argentina. He died on

iv.   03 June 1937 in Buenos Aires, Argentina.

GIOVANNI PEREGO (Marta Chiodera, Carlo Chiodera) was born in 1835. He died on 16 Dec 1914 in Chiavenna, Sondrio, Lombardia, Italy. He married OLIMPIA RIVA.

Giovanni Perego and Olimpia Riva had the following children:

i.   CARLOTTA PEREGO. She married LUIGI CARUGATI in Milano, Lombardia, Italy.

ii.   DUILIO PEREGO. He married RITA MORO in Chiavenna, Sondrio, Lombardia, Italy.

iii. MAMELI PEREGO. He married MARIA LINA DELLA BELLA in Sondrio, Lombardia, Italy.

iv.   MARGHERITA PEREGO. She married ALESSANDRO AUREGGI in Chiavenna, Sondrio, Lombardia, Italy.

Generation 4

MARÍA ANGELINA GANDOLLA (Catherina Perego, Marta Chiodera, Carlo Chiodera) was born on 23 Jun 1877 in Rosario, Santa Fé, Argentina. She died on 25 Jul 1962 in Córdoba, Argentina. She married CARLOS HEINRICH STIEFEL, son of Karl Wilhelm Stiefel and Bertha Angelika Tschuy on 14 Nov 1894 in Carlos Pellegrini, Santa Fé, Argentina. He was born on 23 Aug 1871 in Cañada del Arbol, Dept. San Gerónimo, Santa Fé, Argentina. He died on 01 Aug 1942 in Villa del Lago, Córdoba, Argentina.

Carlos Heinrich Stiefel and María Angelina Gandolla had the following children:

i.   OTILIA ENRIQUETA STIEFEL was born on 10 Aug 1895 in Carlos Pellegrini, Santa Fé, Argentina. She died in 1970 in Santa Fé, Argentina. Became a nun.

ii.   OLIVER STIEFEL was born on 01 May 1907 in Pascanas, Córdoba, Argentina.
      Notes for Oliver Stiefel: We know when he was born, but not when he died. We know of some baby who died in Pascanas and that in the cemetery there was a plaque and that Carlos H. and María were always going carrying flowers on the Day of all the Dead. According to writings in the Diario de la Estancia "Alto Alegre".

iii. ORMANDO CARLOS STIEFEL was born on 10 Apr 1897 in Carlos Pellegrini, Santa Fé, Argentina. He died on 19 Apr 1941, Bajo Chico, Santa María, Córdoba, Argentina. He married JUANA ISABEL SOSA, daughter of Manuel Sosa and María Jaúregui on 07 Dec 1925 in Laborde, Córdoba, Argentina. She was born about 1896 in Pergamino, Buenos Aires, Argentina. She died circa 1982.

iv.   OFELIA CARMEN STIEFEL was born on 13 Apr 1899 in Carlos Pellegrini, Santa Fé, Argentina. She died on 24 Jan 1969 in Córdoba, Argentina. She married ENRIQUE GONZÁLEZ ALBARRACÍN 05 Jun 1922 in Rosario, Santa Fé, Argentina. He was born on 11 Sep 1895. He died on 07 Jul 1969 in Córdoba, Argentina.

v.   OSCAR GUILLERMO STIEFEL was born on 04 Apr 1901 in Carlos Pellegrini, Santa Fé, Argentina. He died on 31 Jul 1986 in Córdoba, Argentina. He married LOLA MARÍA INSÚA, daughter of Feliciano Saúl Insúa and Dolores Harguindey on 17 Feb 1936 in Buenos Aires, Argentina. She was born on 17 Jan 1914 in Chivilcoy, Buenos Aires, Argentina. She died on 04 Nov 2003 in Córdoba, Argentina.

vi.   OCTAVIO ARÍSTIDES STIEFEL was born on 11 Apr 1903 in Rosario, Santa Fé, Argentina. He died on 19 Mar 1991 in Córdoba, Argentina. Became a Jesuit priest.

vii. OTTO MARIO STIEFEL was born on 19 Apr 1905 in Pascanas, Córdoba, Argentina. He died on 07 Nov 1986 in Córdoba, Argentina. He married MARIA RITA CASTELLANO. She was born on 08 Nov 1905. She died on 24 Mar 1997 in Córdoba, Argentina.

CARLOTTA PEREGO (Giovanni Perego, Marta Chiodera, Carlo Chiodera, Giovanni Perego, Giovanni Perego, Francesco Perego). She married LUIGI CARUGATI in Milano, Lombardia, Italy.

Luigi Carugati and Carlotta Perego had the following children:

i.   GIOVANNI CARUGATI.

ii.   CARLA CARUGATI.

DUILIO PEREGO (Giovanni Perego, Marta Chiodera, Carlo Chiodera, Giovanni Perego, Giovanni Perego, Francesco Perego). He married RITA MORO in Chiavenna, Sondrio, Lombardia, Italy.

Duilio Perego and Rita Moro had the following child:

i.   GIOVANNI PEREGO. He married EMMA GRATIROLA in Chiavenna, Sondrio, Lombardia, Italy.

MAMELI PEREGO (Giovanni Perego, Marta Chiodera, Carlo Chiodera, Giovanni Perego, Giovanni Perego, Francesco Perego). He married MARIA LINA DELLA BELLA in Sondrio, Lombardia, Italy.

Mameli Perego and Maria Lina Della Bella had the following children:

i.   EUGENIA PEREGO. She married A. CAWTON.

ii.   GRAZIELLA PEREGO. She married G. DOLCI in Sondrio, Lombardia, Italy.

MARGHERITA Perego (Giovanni Perego, Marta Chiodera, Carlo Chiodera, Giovanni Perego, Giovanni Perego, Francesco Perego). She married ALESSANDRO AUREGGI in Chiavenna, Sondrio, Lombardia, Italy.

Alessandro Aureggi and Margherita Perego had the following child:

i.   OLYMPIA AUREGGI. She married FRANCESCO ARRIATTA.

Generation 5

ORMANDO CARLOS STIEFEL (María Angelina Gandolla, Catherina Perego, Marta Chiodera, Carlo Chiodera) was born 10 Apr 1897 in Carlos Pellegrini, Santa Fé, Argentina. He died 19 Apr 1941, Bajo Chico, Santa María, Córdoba, Argentina. He married JUANA ISABEL SOSA, daughter of Manuel Sosa and María Jaúregui 07 Dec 1925 in Laborde, Córdoba, Argentina. She was born on 23 March 1896 in Pergamino, Buenos Aires, Argentina. She died circa 1982.

Ormando Carlos Stiefel and Juana Isabel Sosa had the following children:

i.   CARLOS FERNANDO STIEFEL was born on 27 Nov 1927 in Laborde, Córdoba, Argentina. He died circa 1927.

ii.   HÉCTOR JUAN MANUEL STIEFEL was born on 15 Nov 1928 in Rio Ceballos, Córdoba, Argentina. He died circa 1928.

iii.   MARÍA ISABEL STIEFEL was born in Sep 1930 in Laborde, Córdoba, Argentina. She married ELISEO VIDELA.

iv.   CARLOS HÉCTOR STIEFEL was born on 30 Dec 1932 in Laborde, Córdoba, Argentina. He died on 18 Nov 1999. He married MARTA MERANO. She was born on 29 Sep 1939. He married PATRICIA GONZÁLEZ.

v.   ELENA SARA STIEFEL was born on 07 Dec 1934 in Pascanas, Córdoba, Argentina. She married JOSE GARIBOTTI.

vi.   LIDIA ESTHER STIEFEL was born on 25 Nov 1935 in Pascanas, Córdoba, Argentina. She died on 20 May 1983 in Córdoba, Argentina. She married ANDRÉS RENE MALPICA. He was born on 20 Nov 1929. He died on 27 Mar 1995 in Córdoba, Argentina.

OFELIA CARMEN STIEFEL (María Angelina Gandolla, Catherina Perego, Marta Chiodera, Carlo Chiodera) was born on 13 Apr 1899 in Carlos Pellegrini, Santa Fé, Argentina. She died on 24 Jan 1969 in Córdoba, Argentina. She married ENRIQUE GONZÁLEZ-ALBARRACÍN on 05 Jun 1922 in Rosario, Santa Fé, Argentina. He was born on 11 Sep 1895. He died on 07 Jul 1969 in Córdoba, Argentina.

Enrique González-Albarracín and Ofelia Carmen Stiefel had the following children:

i.   OFELIA NÉLIDA GONZÁLEZ-ALBARRACÍN was born on 16 Mar 1924. She married IGNACIO VÉLEZ-FUNES.

ii. HELVIA ESTER GONZÁLEZ-ALBARRACÍN was born on 24 Apr 1925. She married MANUEL MARIANO.

iii. ENRIQUE ALBERTO GONZÁLEZ-ALBARRACÍN was born on 24 Jul 1926 in Pascanas, Córdoba, Argentina. He died on 11 Jun 1951. He married MARTA ALLENDE.

iv. JORGE RAÚL GONZÁLEZ-ALBARRACÍN was born on 08 Jan 1928 in Córdoba, Argentina. He married NELLY VALDEZ.

v.   CARLOS IVÁN GONZÁLEZ-ALBARRACÍN was born on 25 Feb 1930. He died on 10 Mar 1991 in Salta, Salta, Argentina. He married MARÍA PIA DEHAUT on 23 Mar 1955 in Unquillo, Córdoba. She was born on 02 Feb 1935 in Buenos Aires, Argentina.

vi   OMAR EMILIO GONZÁLEZ-ALBARRACÍN was born on 08 May 1934. He died on 27 Jul 2000. He married ELVIRA TERESA SOLARI.

vii. SUSANA DEL CARMEN GONZÁLEZ-ALBARRACÍN was born on 21 Sept 1936. She married ERNESTO CARREÑO.

viii. MIRTA TERESA GONZÁLEZ-ALBARRACÍN was born on 13 Dec 1941. She married ALFREDO VILLAGRA.

OSCAR GUILLERMO STIEFEL (María Angelina Gandolla, Catherina Perego, Marta Chiodera, Carlo Chiodera) was born on 04 Apr 1901 in Carlos Pellegrini, Santa Fé, Argentina. He died on 31 Jul 1986 in Córdoba, Argentina. He married LOLA MARÍA INSÚA, daughter of Feliciano Saúl Insúa and Dolores Harguindey on 17 Feb 1936 in Buenos Aires, Argentina. She was born on 17 Jan 1914 in Chivilcoy, Buenos Aires, Argentina. She died on 04 Nov 2003 in Córdoba, Argentina.
Notes for Oscar Guillermo Stiefel: In the documents it appears with those names, but he always said that the third was Christian for his godfather.

Oscar Guillermo Stiefel and Lola María Insúa had the following children:

i.   MARTA BEATRIZ CATALINA STIEFEL was born on 01 Jun 1937 in Buenos Aires, Argentina. She married REYNALDO AYALA on 08 Jun 1958 in Minneapolis, Anoka, Minnesota, USA. He was born on 28 Sep 1934 in Saltillo, Coahuila, Mexico.

ii. MARINA CLARA STIEFEL was born on 01 Dec 1939 in Buenos Aires, Argentina. She married BILL HOY. He was born in the USA.

iii. MARÍA OFELIA STIEFEL was born on 13 Apr 1941. Not married.

iv. OSCAR FELICIANO CARLOS STIEFEL was born on 31 May 1942 in Buenos Aires, Argentina. He married (1) ANA MARÍA RAMONDA, daughter of José Ramonda and Angela Barello   on 10 Jun 1966 in Córdoba, Argentina. She was born on 17 Oct 1944 in Venado Tuerto, Santa Fé, Argentina. He married (2) PATRICIA INÉS MIR, daughter of Juan Carlos Lorenzo Mir and Magdalena María Josefina Mullin on 12 Jun 1999. She was born on 17 Mar 1956 in Buenos Aires, Argentina

OTTO MARIO STIEFEL (María Angelina Gandolla, Catherina Perego, Marta Chiodera, Carlo Chiodera) was born on 19 Apr 1905 in Pascanas, Córdoba, Argentina. He died on 07 Nov 1986 in Córdoba, Argentina. He married MARIA RITA CASTELLANO. She was born on 08 Nov 1905. She died on 24 Mar 1997 in Córdoba, Argentina.

Otto Mario Stiefel and María Rita Castellano had the following children:

i.   MARÍA TERESA STIEFEL was born on 28 Apr 1930 in Villa Dolores, Córdoba, Argentina. She died on 25 Oct 2010 in Córdoba, Argentina. She married ALBERTO PIZARRO.

ii.   RAÚL ADOLFO STIEFEL was born on 24 May 1931 in Pascanas, Córdoba, Argentina. He died on 01 Aug 2010 in Córdoba, Argentina. He married DIANA DE VÉRTIZ on 02 Sep 1961. She was born on 28 Jul 1937.

iii.   BEATRIZ RITA STIEFEL was born on 07 Jun 1932 in Pascanas, Córdoba, Argentina. She married JOSÉ BECERRA.

iv.   SUSANA DEL CARMEN STIEFEL was born on 11 Jan 1935 in Pascanas, Córdoba, Argentina. She married JOSÉ FRANCISCO TORRES on 09 Jan 1959 in Capuchinos, Córdoba.

v.   NOEMÍ LIDIA STIEFEL was born on 21 Sep 1938 in Pascanas, Córdoba, Argentina. She married RAÚL ORIAS.

vi.   OTTO CARLOS STIEFEL was born on 05 Aug 1940 in Pascanas, Córdoba, Argentina. He married HAYDEE NÉLIDA ARCA. She was born on 18 Oct 1939 in Puerto Bermejo, Chaco, Argentina. He married JULIA HORTENSIA YEDRO. She was born on 11 Sep 1955 in Santa Rosa de Calamuchita, Córdoba, Argentina.

vii.   MARÍA RITA STIEFEL was born on 21 Nov 1941. She married JOSE E

viii.   MARÍA LUISA STIEFEL was born on 27 Nov 1942. She married CARLOS GORROCHATEGUI. He was born on 24 Dec 1941.

ix.   MARÍA EUGENIA STIEFEL was born on 28 Nov 1945. She married TONO CASELLA.

GIOVANNI PEREGO (Duilio Perego, Giovanni Perego, Marta Chiodera, Carlo Chiodera, Duilio Perego, Giovanni Perego, Giovanni Perego, Francesco Perego). He married EMMA GRATIROLA in Chiavenna, Sondrio, Lombardia, Italy.

Giovanni Perego and Emma Gratirola had the following child:

i.   MARTA PEREGO.

EUGENIA PEREGO (Mameli Perego, Giovanni Perego, Marta Chiodera, Carlo Chiodera, Mameli Perego, Giovanni Perego, Giovanni Perego, Francesco Perego). She married A. CAWTON.

A. Cawton and Eugenia Perego had the following child:

i.   MARIA PAOLA CAWTON

GRAZIELLA PEREGO (Mameli Perego, Giovanni Perego, Marta Chiodera, Carlo Chiodera, Mameli Perego, Giovanni Perego, Giovanni Perego, Francesco Perego). She married G. DOLCI in Sondrio, Lombardia, Italy.

G. Dolci and Graziella Perego had the following children:

i.   ALBERTO DOLCI
ii.   RENATO DOLCI

OLYMPIA AUREGGI (Margherita Perego, Giovanni Perego, Marta Chiodera, Carlo Chiodera, Alessandro Aureggi). She married FRANCESCO ARRIATTA.

Francesco Arriatta and Olympia Aureggi had the following child:

i.   MARGHERITTA ARRIATTA.

Generation 6

MARÍA ISABEL STIEFEL (Ormando Carlos, María Angelina Gandolla, Catherina Perego, Marta Chiodera, Carlo Chiodera) was born in Sep 1930 in Laborde, Córdoba, Argentina. She married ELISEO VIDELA.

Eliseo Videla and Maria Isabel Stiefel had the following children:

i.   FLAVIA VIDELA. She married EDUARDO GOMEZ.
ii.   ELISEO VIDELA. He married GERTRUDIS ZECHNER.
iii.   FABIÁN VIDELA was born on 02 Oct 1959 in Córdoba, Argentina. He married CAROLINA ABBONA. She was born on 01 Nov 1964
vi.   MERCEDES VIDELA was born in 1970. She married JUAN M. ZARAZAGA

CARLOS HÉCTOR STIEFEL (Ormando Carlos, María Angelina Gandolla, Catherina Perego, Marta Chiodera, Carlo Chiodera) was born on 30 Dec 1932 in Laborde, Córdoba, Argentina. He died on 18 Nov 1999. He married MARTA MERANO. She was born on 29 Sep 1939. He married PATRICIA GONZÁLEZ. He married PATRICIA GONZÁLEZ.

Carlos Héctor Stiefel and Marta Merano had the following children:

i.   GERMÁN CARLOS STIEFEL was born on 07 Feb 1956 (Bajo Chico, Santa María, Córdoba, Argentina). He married EMILCE BEATRIZ FLORES. She was born on 28 Dec 1955.

ii.   GUSTAVO STIEFEL was born on 06 Aug 1957 in Alta Gracia, Córdoba, Argentina. He married MARINA LABOMBARDA. She was born on 13 Jan 1977 in Buenos Aires, Argentina.

iii.   SERGIO STIEFEL

Carlos Héctor Stiefel and Patricia González had the following children:

i.   MARIANO STIEFEL.
ii.   GUILLERMO STIEFEL.
iii.   ORMANDO STIEFEL.
iv.   NATALIA STIEFEL.

ELENA SARA STIEFEL (Ormando Carlos, María Angelina Gandolla, Catherina Perego, Marta Chiodera, Carlo Chiodera) was born on 07 Dec 1934 in Pascanas, Córdoba, Argentina. She married JOSE GARIBOTTI.

José Garibotti and Elena Sara Stiefel had the following children:

i.   FEDERICO GARIBOTTI. He married KELLY FLORIT.
ii.   CAROLA GARIBOTTI. She married MARIO RUA.
iii.   FLORENCIA GARIBOTTI.

LIDIA ESTHER STIEFEL (Ormando Carlos, María Angelina Gandolla, Catherina Perego, Marta Chiodera, Carlo Chiodera) was born on 25 Nov 1935 in Pascanas, Córdoba, Argentina. She died on 20 May 1983 in Córdoba, Argentina. She married ANDRÉS RENE MALPICA. He was born on 20 Nov 1929. He died on 27 Mar 1995 in Córdoba, Argentina.

Andrés Rene Malpica and Lidia Esther Stiefel had the following children:

i.   ANDRÉS DANIEL MALPICA was born on 03 Mar 1962.
ii.   MARIELA MALPICA was born on 25 Jul 1963. She married PABLO TRAVERSO. He was born on 28 Apr 1960.
iii.   MAURICIO ORMANDO MALPICA was born on 23 Oct 1964. He married EMILY SCHNEBLY. She was born on 13 Mar 1963. He married AMY BURLINGHAME. She was born on 22 Aug 1965.
iv.   CONSTANZA MALPICA was born on 09 Oct 1968. She married EDGARDO JOSÉ SOSA. He was born on 17 Jun 1958.

OFELIA NÉLIDA GONZÁLEZ-ALBARRACÍN (Ofelia Carmen Stiefel, María Angelina Gandolla, Catherina Perego, Marta Chiodera, Carlo Chiodera) was born on 16 Mar 1924. She married IGNACIO VÉLEZ-FUNES

Ignacio Vélez-Funes and Ofelia Nélida González-Albarracín had the following children:

i.   IGNACIO VÉLEZ-FUNES. He married VICTORIA PAGANINI.
ii.   OFELIA MARÍA VÉLEZ-FUNES was born on 04 Nov 1950. She married FERNANDO AVILA.
iii.   LUIS VÉLEZ-FUNES. He married NILDA FERRER-VIEYRA.
iv.   JOSÉ VÉLEZ-FUNES.
v.   JUAN CARLOS VÉLEZ-FUNES. He married REYNA.

HELVIA ESTER GONZÁLEZ-ALBARRACÍN (Ofelia Carmen Stiefel, María Angelina Gandolla, Catherina Perego, Marta Chiodera, Carlo Chiodera) was born on 24 Apr 1925. She married MANUEL MARIANO.

Manuel Mariano and Helvia Ester González-Albarracín had the following children:

i.   TERESITA ADRIANA MARIANO was born in May 1947. She died in Aug 1992. She married ENZO RÉBORA
ii.   MANUEL MARIANO. He married SUSANA CANEDO.
iii.   MARÍA ALEJANDRA MARIANO. She married JORGE VISCONTI.

iv.   PABLO MARIANO was born on 20 Jan 1953. He married PITI CLARIÁ.

ENRIQUE ALBERTO GONZÁLEZ-ALBARRACÍN (Ofelia Carmen Stiefel, María Angelina Gandolla, Catherina Perego, Marta Chiodera, Carlo Chiodera) was born 24 Jul 1926 in Pascanas, Córdoba, Argentina. He died on 11 Jun 1951. He married MARTA ALLENDE.

Enrique Alberto González-Albarracín and Marta Allende had the following child:
i.   MARTA GONZÁLEZ-ALBARRACÍN. She married CONSTANTINO SANTURIO

CARLOS IVÁN GONZÁLEZ-ALBARRACÍN (Ofelia Carmen Stiefel, María Angelina Gandolla, Catherina Perego, Marta Chiodera, Carlo Chiodera) was born 25 Feb 1930. He died on 10 Mar 1991 in Salta, Salta, Argentina. He married MARÍA PÍA DEHAUT on 23 Mar 1955 in Unquillo, Córdoba. She was born on 02 Feb 1935 in Buenos Aires, Argentina.

Carlo González-Albarracín and María Pía Dehaut had the following child:
i.   CARLOS GONZÁLEZ-ALBARRACÍN was born on 14 Dec 1955. He married LUCÍA
        WETZEL. She was born on 07 Oct 1958.

OMAR EMILIO GONZÁLEZ-ALBARRACÍN (Ofelia Carmen Stiefel, María Angelina Gandolla, Catherina Perego, Marta Chiodera, Carlo Chiodera) was born on 08 May 1934. He died 27 Jul 2000. He married ELVIRA TERESA SOLARI.

Omar Emilio González-Albarracín and Elvira Teresa Solari had the following children:
i.   CAROLINA GONZÁLEZ-ALBARRACÍN. She married JUAN MANUEL
        DUPUY.
ii.   JULIO GONZÁLEZ-ALBARRACÍN. He married CAROLINA BUFFADORI.
iii.   GUSTAVO GONZÁLEZ-ALBARRACÍN. He married MÓNICA
        HINTERWIMMER.
iv.   MARCELA GONZÁLEZ-ALBARRACÍN. She married DANIEL FRUTOS.
v.   SOFIA GONZÁLEZ-ALBARRACÍN

SUSANA DEL CARMEN GONZÁLEZ-ALBARRACÍN (Ofelia Carmen Stiefel, María Angelina Gandolla, Catherina Perego, Marta Chiodera, Carlo Chiodera) was born on 21 Sep 1936. She married ERNESTO CARREÑO.

Ernesto Carreño and Susana del Carmen González-Albarracín had the following children:
i.   ALEJANDRO CARREÑO. He married INES COLOME.
ii.   Pablo CARREÑO. He married María Eugenia Estario on 12 May 1995
iii.   OFELIA CARREÑO
iv.   ERNESTO CARREÑO
v.   MARCOS CARREÑO.

MIRTA TERESA GONZÁLEZ-ALBARRACÍN (Ofelia Carmen Stiefel, María Angelina Gandolla, Catherina Perego, Marta Chiodera, Carlo Chiodera) was born on 13 Dec 1941. She married ALFREDO VILLAGRA.

Alfredo Villagra and Mirta Teresa González-Albarracín had the following children:

i.   MARÍA BELÉN VILLAGRA. She married ELIO CURET.
ii.   ALFREDO JOSE VILLAGRA. He married ANDREA CURBELO.
iii.   SOLEDAD VILLAGRA. She married FÉLIX OLMEDO.
iv.   CECILIA VILLAGRA.

MARTA BEATRIZ CATALINA STIEFEL (Oscar Guillermo, María Angelina Gandolla, Catherina Perego, Marta Chiodera, Carlo Chiodera) was born on 01 Jun 1937 in Buenos Aires, Argentina. She married REYNALDO AYALA on 08 Jun 1958 in Minneapolis, Anoka, Minnesota, USA. He was born on 28 Sep 1934 in Saltillo, Coahuila, Mexico.

Reynaldo Ayala and Marta Beatriz Catalina Stiefel had the following children:

i.   CARLOS CUAUHTEMOC AYALA was born on 26 Apr 1960 in Minneapolis, Anoka, Minnesota, USA. He married MARY ANN MACEVICZ on 05 Nov 1988 in San Diego, California, USA. She was born on 25 Nov 1958.
ii.   GUADALUPE XOCHITL AYALA was born on 27 Dec 1962 in Carbondale, Jackson, Illinois, USA. She married DANE TOVEY on 18 Jan 1992 in San Diego, California. He was born on 25 Jul 1950 in Danville, Vermilion, Illinois, USA.
iii.   EMILIANO CUITLAHUAC AYALA was born on 08 Sep 1964 in Carbondale, Jackson, Illinois, USA. He married CATHERINE ANNE SHEHAN on 17 Jul 1990.

MARINA CLARA STIEFEL (Oscar Guillermo, María Angelina Gandolla, Catherina Perego, Marta Chiodera, Carlo Chiodera) was born 01 Dec 1939 in Buenos Aires, Argentina. She married BILL HOY. He was born in USA.

Bill Hoy and Marina Clara Stiefel had the following child:

i.   ADRIANA HOY was born on 16 May 1981 in USA. She married SHAUN RYAN KLANSNIC on 06 May 2004. He was born on 21 May 1978 in USA.

OSCAR FELICIANO CARLOS STIEFEL (Oscar Guillermo, María Angelina Gandolla, Catherina Perego, Marta Chiodera, Carlo Chiodera) was born on 31 May 1942 in Buenos Aires, Argentina. He married (1) ANA MARÍA RAMONDA, daughter of José Ramonda and Angela Barello on 10 Jun 1966 in Córdoba, Argentina. She was born on 17 Oct 1944 in Venado Tuerto, Santa Fé, Argentina. He married (2) PATRICIA INÉS MIR, daughter of Juan Carlos Lorenzo Mir and Magdalena María Joséfina Mullin on 12 Jun 1999. She was born on 17 Mar 1956 in Buenos Aires, Argentina.

Oscar Feliciano Carlos Stiefel and Ana María Ramonda had the following children:

i.   GUSTAVO OSCAR STIEFEL was born on 24 Jun 1967 in Córdoba, Argentina.

ii.   CRISTIAN GUILLERMO STIEFEL was born on 11 Aug 1969 in Córdoba, Argentina. He married LUISINA FREITES.

iii.   LUCAS CARLOS STIEFEL was born on 03 May 1975 in Córdoba, Argentina. He married INGRID DELLS.

iv.   BÁRBARA STIEFEL was born on 14 Jul 1977 in Córdoba, Argentina. She met MARIANO ACOSTA.

MARÍA TERESA STIEFEL (Otto Mario, María Angelina Gandolla, Catherina Perego, Marta Chiodera, Carlo Chiodera) was born on 28 Apr 1930 in Villa Dolores, Córdoba, Argentina. She . She died on 25 Oct 2010 in Córdoba, Argentina. She married ALBERTO PIZARRO.

Alberto Pizarro and María Teresa Stiefel had the following children:

i.   LUIS ALBERTO PIZARRO.

ii.   ENRIQUE PIZARRO.

iii.   MARIA TERESA PIZARRO. She married ERNESTO A.

iv.   MARIA PIA PIZARRO.

v.   MARIA CECILIA PIZARRO. She married FERNANDEZ.

vi.   JOSE IGNACIO PIZARRO.

vii.   RUTH PIZARRO.

viii.   FERNANDO PIZARRO.

RAÚL ADOLFO STIEFEL (Otto Mario, María Angelina Gandolla, Catherina Perego, Marta Chiodera, Carlo Chiodera) was born on 24 May 1931 in Pascanas, Córdoba, Argentina. He died on 01 Aug 2010 in Córdoba, Argentina. He married DIANA DE VÉRTIZ on 02 Sep 1961. She was born on 28 Jul 1937.

Raúl Adolfo Stiefel and Diana de Vértiz had the following children:

i.   RAÚL ANDRÉS STIEFEL was born on 17 Jun 1962. He married ADRIANA PATRICIA MIANI on 10 Mar 1990. She was born on 19 Sep 1964.

ii.   MARIANA STIEFEL was born on 25 Jan 1965 in Córdoba, Argentina.

iii.   CAROLINA STIEFEL was born on 26 Mar 1966. She married JORGE JOFRÉ.

iv.   EUGENIO STIEFEL was born on 06 Jul 1963 in Córdoba, Argentina. He died on 03 Mar 2007 in Córdoba, Argentina.

v.   MARCOS STIEFEL was born in 1968. He married PAULA DEL VISO. She was born in 1973.

vi.   DIANA STIEFEL. She married HORACIO VILLADA.

vii.   CONSTANZA STIEFEL. She married JUAN GNARA.

BEATRIZ RITA STIEFEL (Otto Mario, María Angelina Gandolla, Catherina Perego, Marta Chiodera, Carlo Chiodera) was born on 07 Jun 1932 in Pascanas, Córdoba, Argentina. She married JOSÉ BECERRA.

José Becerra and Beatriz Rita Stiefel had the following children:

i. RODOLFO BECERRA.

ii. ALEJANDRO BECERRA.

iii. PABLO BECERRA.

iv. FRANCISCO JOSÉ BECERRA. He married CONSUELO GUTIERREZ-RIUS.

v. BEATRIZ BECERRA was born on 12 Sep 1964. She married LUIS MANZANARES.

vi AGUSTIN BECERRA.

vii. CLARA ROSA BECERRA.

SUSANA DEL CARMEN STIEFEL (Otto Mario, María Angelina Gandolla, Catherina Perego, Marta Chiodera, Carlo Chiodera) was born on 11 Jan 1935 in Pascanas, Córdoba, Argentina. She married JOSE FRANCISCO TORRES on 09 Jan 1959 in Capuchinos, Córdoba.

José Francisco Torres and Susana del Carmen Stiefel had the following children:

i. SUSANA DEL CARMEN TORRES was born on 30 Oct 1959 in Córdoba, Argentina. She married JUAN CARLOS ALVAREZ.

ii. INES MARIA TORRES. She married JAVIER NIEVAS.

iii. JOSE FRANCISCO TORRES was born on 18 Dec 1963. He married AMY GIL.

iv. MARIA ALEJANDRA TORRES was born on 20 Jul 1965.

NOEMÍ LIDIA STIEFEL (Otto Mario, María Angelina Gandolla, Catherina Perego, Marta Chiodera, Carlo Chiodera) was born on 21 Sep 1938 in Pascanas, Córdoba, Argentina. He married RAÚL ORIAS.

Raúl Orias and Noemí Lidia Stiefel had the following children:

i. FERNAND ORIAS.

ii. MARCELO ORIAS. He married SUSANA FERRER.

iii. RAQUEL ORIAS.

OTTO CARLOS STIEFEL (Otto Mario, María Angelina Gandolla, Catherina Perego, Marta Chiodera, Carlo Chiodera) was born on 05 Aug 1940 in Pascanas, Córdoba, Argentina. He married HAYDEE NÉLIDA ARCA. She was born on 18 Oct 1939 in Puerto Bermejo, Chaco, Argentina. He married JULIA HORTENSIA YEDRO. She was born on 11 Sep 1955 in Santa Rosa de Calamuchita, Córdoba, Argentina.

Otto Carlos Stiefel and Haydee Nélida Arca had the following children:

i. VALERIA M. STIEFEL. She married GUSTAVO CROSETTO.

ii. LUCRECIA STIEFEL. She married GUSTAVO YUNES.

iii. JOSEFINA STIEFEL. She married JOSÉ MANUEL GARCIA on 30 Apr 1999.

iv. OTTO STIEFEL.

Otto Carlos Stiefel and Julia Hortensia Yedro had the following child:

i.   SANTIAGO ARIEL STIEFEL was born on 03 Mar 1994 in Santa Rosa de Calamuchita, Córdoba, Argentina.

MARÍA RITA STIEFEL (Otto Mario, María Angelina Gandolla, Catherina Perego, Marta Chiodera, Carlo Chiodera) was born on 21 Nov 1941. She married JOSE EGUIA.

José Eguía and María Rita Stiefel had the following children:

i.   EUGENIA EGUIA.
ii.   JOSE EGUIA.
iii.   CECILIA EGUIA.

MARÍA LUISA STIEFEL (Otto Mario María Angelina Gandolla, Catherina Perego, Marta Chiodera, Carlo Chiodera) was born on 27 Nov 1942. She married CARLOS GORROCHATEGUI. He was born on 24 Dec 1941.

Carlos Gorrochategui and María Luisa Stiefel had the following children:

i.   MAGDALENA GORROCHATEGUI was born on 01 Jan 1969. She married PABLO REVOLA.
ii.   CELINA GORROCHATEGUI was born on 13 Mar 1970. She married OSCAR RUIZ LUQUE.
iii.   ESTEBAN GORROCHATEGUI was born on 25 Feb 1971. He married CONSUELO NORES.
iv.   INES GORROCHATEGUI was born on 13 Jun 1973. She married GUSTAVO OLIVA.

MARÍA EUGENIA STIEFEL (Otto Mario, María Angelina Gandolla, Catherina Perego, Marta Chiodera, Carlo Chiodera) was born on 28 Nov 1945. She married TONO CASELLA.

Tono Casella and María Eugenia Stiefel had the following children:

i.   NICOLAS CASELLA.
ii.   FLORENCIA CASELLA.
iii.   MARTIN CASELLA.

Generation 7

FLAVIA VIDELA (María Isabel Stiefel, Ormando Carlos Stiefel, María Angelina Gandolla, Catherina Perego, Marta Chiodera, Carlo Chiodera, Eliseo Videla). She married EDUARDO GOMEZ.

Eduardo Gomez and Flavia Videla had the following child:

i.   CONSTANZA GOMEZ.

ELISEO VIDELA (María Isabel Stiefel, Ormando Carlos Stiefel, María Angelina Gandolla, Catherina Perego, Marta Chiodera, Carlo Chiodera, Eliseo Videla). He married GERTRUDIS ZECHNER.

Eliseo Videla and Gertrudis Zechner had the following children:
i.   PAULA VIDELA.
ii.   ELISEO VIDELA.
iii.   LUCAS VIDELA.

FABIÁN VIDELA (María Isabel Stiefel, Ormando Carlos Stiefel, María Angelina Gandolla, Catherina Perego, Marta Chiodera, Carlo Chiodera) was born on 02 Oct 1959 in Córdoba, Argentina. He married CAROLINA ABBONA. She was born on 01 Nov 1964.

Fabián Videla and Carolina Abbona had the following children:
i.   VALENTINA VIDELA was born on 13 Jun 1991.
ii.   MAURICIO GUIDO VIDELA was born on 23 Apr 1993.
iii.   FACUNDO VIDELA was born on 06 Dec 1995.

MERCEDES VIDELA (María Isabel Stiefel, Ormando Carlos Stiefel, María Angelina Gandolla, Catherina Perego, Marta Chiodera, Carlo Chiodera) was born in 1970. She married JUAN M. ZARAZAGA.

Juan M. Zarazaga and Mercedes Videla had the following children:
i.   EMILIA ZARAZAGA.
ii.   ROCÍO ZARAZAGA
iii.   CLARA ZARAZAGA.

GERMÁN CARLOS STIEFEL (Carlos Héctor, Ormando Carlos, María Angelina Gandolla, Catherina Perego, Marta Chiodera, Carlo Chiodera) was born on 07 Feb 1956 (Bajo Chico, Santa María, Córdoba, Argentina). He married EMILCE BEATRIZ FLORES. She was born on 28 Dec 1955.

Germán Carlos Stiefel and Emilce Beatriz Flores had the following children:
i.   IVANA STIEFEL was born on 19 Sep 1979 in Alta Gracia, Córdoba, Argentina.
ii.   SABRINA STIEFEL was born in Alta Gracia, Córdoba, Argentina.
iii.   LUCAS STIEFEL was born in Alta Gracia, Córdoba, Argentina.

GUSTAVO STIEFEL (Carlos Héctor, Ormando Carlos, María Angelina Gandolla, Catherina Perego, Marta Chiodera, Carlo Chiodera) was born on 06 Aug 1957 in Alta Gracia, Córdoba, Argentina. He married MARINA LABOMBARDA. She was born on 13 Jan 1977 in Buenos Aires, Argentina.

Gustavo Stiefel and Marina Labombarda had the following child:

i.   EXEQUIEL LABOMBARDA was born on 01 Dec 1995 in Alta Gracia, Córdoba, Argentina.

FEDERICO GARIBOTTI (Elena Sara Stiefel, Ormando Carlos Stiefel, María Angelina Gandolla, Catherina Perego, Marta Chiodera, Carlo Chiodera, Jose Garibotti). He married KELLY FLORIT.

Federico Garibotti and Kelly Florit had the following children:

i.   VALENTINA GARIBOTTI.
ii.   JOSE JUAN GARIBOTTI.
iii.   FELIPE GARIBOTTI.

CAROLA GARIBOTTI (Elena Sara Stiefel, Ormando Carlos Stiefel, María Angelina Gandolla, Catherina Perego, Marta Chiodera, Carlo Chiodera, Jose Garibotti). She married MARIO RUA.

Mario Rua and Carola Garibotti had the following children:

i.   FRANCISCO RUA.
ii.   PEDRO RUA.

MARIELA MALPICA (Lidia Esther Stiefel, Ormando Carlos Stiefel, María Angelina Gandolla, Catherina Perego, Marta Chiodera, Carlo Chiodera) was born on 25 Jul 1963. She married PABLO TRAVERSO. He was born on 28 Apr 1960.

Pablo Traverso and Mariela Malpica had the following children:

i.   MALENA TRAVERSO was born on 14 Nov 1984.
ii.   PABLO TRAVERSO was born on 26 Dec 1986.

MAURICIO ORMANDO MALPICA (Lidia Esther Stiefel, Ormando Carlos Stiefel, María Angelina Gandolla, Catherina Perego, Marta Chiodera, Carlo Chiodera) was born on 23 Oct 1964. He married EMILY SCHNEBLY. She was born on 13 Mar 1963. He married AMY BURLINGHAME. She was born on 22 Aug 1965.

Mauricio Ormando Malpica and Emily Schnebly had the following child:

i.   TZEGA MALPICA was born on 28 Oct 1987.

Mauricio Ormando Malpica and Amy Burlinghame had the following children:

i.   MARCELINO MALPICA was born on 24 Sep 1993.
ii.   SALVADOR MALPICA was born on 07 Dec 1997.

CONSTANZA MALPICA (Lidia Esther Stiefel, Ormando Carlos Stiefel, María Angelina Gandolla, Catherina Perego, Marta Chiodera, Carlo Chiodera) was born on 09 Oct 1968. She married EDGARDO JOSÉ SOSA. He was born on 17 Jun 1958.

Edgardo José Sosa and Constanza Malpica had the following children:

i.   EMA SOSA was born on 02 Aug 1999.

ii.   MATEO JOSÉ SOSA was born on 16 Sep 2002.

IGNACIO VÉLEZ-FUNES (Ofelia Nélida González-Albarracín, Ofelia Carmen Stiefel, María Angelina Gandolla, Catherina Perego, Marta Chiodera, Carlo Chiodera, Ignacio Vélez-Funes). He married VICTORIA PAGANINI.

Ignacio Vélez-Funes and Victoria Paganini had the following children:

i.   IGNACIO VÉLEZ-FUNES.

ii.   LUCRECIA VÉLEZ-FUNES.

ii.   VICTORIA VÉLEZ-FUNES.

OFELIA MARÍA VÉLEZ-FUNES (Ofelia Nélida González-Albarracín, Ofelia Carmen Stiefel, María Angelina Gandolla, Catherina Perego, Marta Chiodera, Carlo Chiodera) was born on 04 Nov 1950. She married FERNANDO AVILA. She married JORGE VISCONTI.

Fernando Avila and Ofelia María Vélez-Funes had the following children:

i.   JUAN FERNANDO AVILA was born on 24 Sep 1975.

ii.   MARÍA VICTORIA AVILA was born on 06 May 1977.

iii.   MAGDALENA AVILA was born on 04 Jan 1979.

iv.   AGUSTÍN AVILA was born on 12 Mar 1982.

LUIS VÉLEZ-FUNES (Ofelia Nélida González-Albarracín, Ofelia Carmen Stiefel, María Angelina Gandolla, Catherina Perego, Marta Chiodera, Carlo Chiodera, Ignacio Vélez-Funes). He married NILDA FERRER-VIEYRA.

Luis Vélez-Funes and Nilda Ferrer-Vieyra had the following children:

i.   SANDRA VÉLEZ-FUNES. She married JUAN JOSE PITT.

ii.   SOFIA VÉLEZ-FUNES. She married GUILLERMO ARIEL ROZZE.

iii.   PILAR VÉLEZ-FUNES. She married PATRICIO JOSE RIVERO.

iv.   LUIS MARIA VÉLEZ-FUNES. He married MARIA ROSE DELIAS.

v.   JAVIER VÉLEZ-FUNES.

vi.   SANTIAGO VÉLEZ-FUNES.

vii.   MARIA NILDA VÉLEZ-FUNES.

viii.   ROCIO VÉLEZ-FUNES. She married PEDRO SOCCONE.

ix.   PEDRO VÉLEZ-FUNES.

TERESITA ADRIANA MARIANO (Helvia Ester González-Albarracín, Ofelia Carmen Stiefel, María Angelina Gandolla, Catherina Perego, Marta Chiodera, Carlo Chiodera) was born in May 1947. She died in Aug 1992. She married ENZO RÉBORA.

Enzo Rébora and Teresita Adriana Mariano had the following children:

i.   PAOLA RÉBORA. She married JOSÉ DEL BOCA.

ii.   TOMAS RÉBORA.

iii.   JUAN RÉBORA.

MANUEL MARIANO (Helvia Ester González-Albarracín, Ofelia Carmen Stiefel, María Angelina Gandolla, Catherina Perego, Marta Chiodera, Carlo Chiodera, Manuel Mariano). He married SUSANA CANEDO.

Manuel Mariano and Susana Canedo had the following children:

i.   CANDELA MARIANO.

ii.   MANUEL MARIANO.

iii.   IGNACIO MARIANO.

MARÍA ALEJANDRA MARIANO (Helvia Ester González-Albarracín, Ofelia Carmen Stiefel, María Angelina Gandolla, Catherina Perego, Marta Chiodera, Carlo Chiodera, Manuel Mariano). She married JORGE VISCONTI.

Jorge Visconti and María Alejandra Mariano had the following children:

i.   GENARO VISCONTI. He married MARINA BOTTA.

ii.   RANCO VISCONTI.

PABLO MARIANO (Helvia Ester González-Albarracín, Ofelia Carmen Stiefel, María Angelina Gandolla, Catherina Perego, Marta Chiodera, Carlo Chiodera) was born on 20 Jan 1953. He married PITI CLARIÁ.

Pablo Mariano and Piti Clariá had the following children:

i.   FLORENCIA MARIANO was born on 30 Apr 1980.

ii.   VICTORIA MARIANO was born on 25 Apr 1985.

iii.   JULIETA MARIANO was born on 26 Sep 1989.

MARTA GONZÁLEZ-ALBARRACÍN (Enrique Alberto González-Albarracin, Ofelia Carmen Stiefel, María Angelina Gandolla, Catherina Perego, Marta Chiodera, Carlo Chiodera). She married CONSTANTINO SANTURIO.

Constantino Santurio and Marta González-Albarracín had the following children:

i.   MARÍA MARTA SANTURIO.

ii.   MARÍA GIMENA SANTURIO.

iii.   MAXIMILIANO JOSÉ SANTURIO.

iv.   MARÍA BELÉN SANTURIO.

v.   SANTIAGO JAVIER SANTURIO.

CARLOS GONZÁLEZ-ALBARRACÍN (Carlos Iván, Ofelia Carmen Stiefel, María Angelina Gandolla, Catherina Perego, Marta Chiodera, Carlo Chiodera) was born on 14 Dec 1955. He married LUCÍA WETZEL. She was born on 07 Oct 1958.

Carlos González-Albarracín and Lucía Wetzel had the following children:
i.   CARLA GONZÁLEZ-ALBARRACÍN.
ii.   JULIA GONZÁLEZ-ALBARRACÍN.
iii. GERMÁN GONZÁLEZ-ALBARRACÍN.

CAROLINA GONZÁLEZ-ALBARRACÍN (Omar Emilio González-Albarracín, Ofelia Carmen Stiefel, María Angelina Gandolla, Catherina Perego, Marta Chiodera, Carlo Chiodera). She married JUAN MANUEL DUPUY.

Juan Manuel Dupuy and Carolina González-Albarracín had the following children:
i.   JULIA DUPUY.
ii.   MANUEL DUPUY.

JULIO GONZÁLEZ-ALBARRACÍN (Omar Emilio González-Albarracín, Ofelia Carmen Stiefel, María Angelina Gandolla, Catherina Perego, Marta Chiodera, Carlo Chiodera). He married CAROLINA BUFFADORI.

Julio González-Albarracín and Carolina Buffadori had the following child:
i.   FEDERICA GONZÁLEZ-ALBARRACÍN.

GUSTAVO GONZÁLEZ-ALBARRACÍN (Omar Emilio González-Albarracín, Ofelia Carmen Stiefel, María Angelina Gandolla, Catherina Perego, Marta Chiodera, Carlo Chiodera). He married MÓNICA HINTERWIMMER.
Gustavo González-Albarracín and Mónica Hinterwimmer had the following child:
i.   SAYA GONZÁLEZ-ALBARRACÍN.

MARCELA GONZÁLEZ-ALBARRACÍN (Omar Emilio González-Albarracín, Ofelia Carmen Stiefel, María Angelina Gandolla, Catherina Perego, Marta Chiodera, Carlo Chiodera). She married DANIEL FRUTOS.

Daniel Frutos and Marcela González-Albarracín had the following children:
i.   DANIEL FRUTOS.
ii.   MARTINO FRUTOS.
iii. JIMENA FRUTOS.
iv.   TOBÍAS FRUTOS.

ALEJANDRO CARREÑO (Susana Del Carmen González-Albarracín, Ofelia Carmen Stiefel, María Angelina Gandolla, Catherina Perego, Marta Chiodera, Carlo Chiodera, Ernesto Carreño). He married INES COLOME.

Alejandro Carreño and Ines Colome had the following children:

i.   LUCAS CARREÑO.

ii.   GASTON CARREÑO.

iii.   PAULA CARREÑO.

PABLO CARREÑO (Susana Del Carmen González-Albarracín, Ofelia Carmen Stiefel, María Angelina Gandolla, Catherina Perego, Marta Chiodera, Carlo Chiodera, Ernesto Carreño). He married MARÍA EUGENIA ESTARIO on 12 May 1995.

Pablo Carreño and María Eugenia Estario had the following children:

i.   JUAN IGNACIO CARREÑO.

ii.   PEDRO MANUEL CARREÑO.

iii.   SANTIAGO IVAN CARREÑO.

MARÍA BELÉN VILLAGRA (Mirta Teresa González-Albarracín, Ofelia Carmen Stiefel, María Angelina Gandolla, Catherina Perego, Marta Chiodera, Carlo Chiodera, Alfredo Villagra). She married ELIO CURET.

Elio Curet and María Belén Villagra had the following children:

i.   HERNÁN CURET.

ii.   LOURDES CURET.

iii.   JOSEFINA CURET.

iv.   BELÉN CURET.

v.   TOMÁS CURE.

SOLEDAD VILLAGRA (Mirta Teresa González-Albarracín, Ofelia Carmen Stiefel, María Angelina Gandolla, Catherina Perego, Marta Chiodera, Carlo Chiodera, Alfredo Villagra). She married FÉLIX OLMEDO.

Félix Olmedo and Soledad Villagra had the following children:

i.   LUCÍA OLMEDO.

ii.   JAVIER OLMEDO.

iii.   ROSARIO OLMEDO.

iv.   FÉLIX OLMEDO.

v.   TOBIAS OLMEDO.

vi.   JOSÉ MARÍA OLMEDO.

CARLOS CUAUHTEMOC AYALA (Marta Beatriz Catalina Stiefel, Oscar Guillermo Stiefel, María Angelina Gandolla, Catherina Perego, Marta Chiodera, Carlo Chiodera) was born on 26 Apr 1960 in Minneapolis, Anoka, Minnesota, USA. He married MARY ANN MACEVICZ on 05 Nov 1988 in San Diego, California, USA. She was born on 25 Nov 1958 in San Diego, CA.

Carlos Cuauhtémoc Ayala and Mary Ann Macevicz had the following children:

i.   MAYA JAZMIN AYALA was born 22 August 1991 in San Diego, CA. She married
        BERNARD P. FERNANDES 10 July 2020. He was born 19 July 1986 in Georgetown, Guyana.

ii.   KENYA CLAVEL AYALA was born in USA. She married ANTHONY JUAN LOPEZ 6
        January 2018. He was born 23 December 1987 in Merced, CA. They changed their last
        name to AYEZ when they got married.

EMILIANO CUITLAHUAC AYALA (Marta Beatriz Catalina Stiefel, Oscar Guillermo Stiefel, María
Angelina Gandolla, Catherina Perego, Marta Chiodera, Carlo Chiodera) was born on 08 Sep 1964 in
Carbondale, Jackson, Illinois, USA. He married CATHERINE ANNE SHEHAN on 17 Jul 1990. She was
born 28 December 1955 in Riverside, CA.

Emiliano Cuitlahuac Ayala and Catherine Anne Shehan had the following children:

i.   NASTASSIA NOELLE AYALA was born on 05 Sep 1991 in Palm Springs, CA. She married
        CODY TRETTIN 18 December 2021. He was born 13 November 1991 in Santa Rosa, CA.

ii.   GISELLE ESME AYALA was born on 12 Jul 1994 in Palm Springs, CA. She died on 05 April
        2013 in Santa Barbara, California, USA (Accident, falling off a cliff at Isla
        Vista during a spring break party).

ADRIANA HOY (Marina Clara Stiefel, Oscar Guillermo Stiefel, María Angelina Gandolla, Catherina
Perego, Marta Chiodera, Carlo Chiodera) was born on 16 May 1981 in Santa Fe, New Mexico. She
married SHAUN RYAN KLANSNIC on 06 May 2004. He was born on 21 May 1978 in Nuremberg,
Germany.

Shaun Ryan Klansnic and Adriana Margarita Hoy had the following children:

i.   EVAN RIAN KLANSNIC was born on 26 May 2004 in Lonetree, Colorado.

ii.   AIDAN XAVIER KLANSNIC was born on 14 May 2006 in Lonetree, Colorado.

iii.   TRISTAN KLANSNIC was born 09 April 2013 in Park City, Utah.

CRISTIAN GUILLERMO STIEFEL (Oscar Feliciano Carlos, Oscar Guillermo, María Angelina Gandolla,
Catherina Perego, Marta Chiodera, Carlo Chiodera) was born on 11 Aug 1969 in Córdoba,
Argentina. He married LUISINA FREITES. She was born 29 November 1982

Cristian Guillermo Stiefel and Luisina Freites had the following child:

i.   GUILLERMO NICOLÁS STIEFEL was born on 20 Dec 2012 in Córdoba, Argentina.

LUCAS CARLOS STIEFEL (Oscar Feliciano Carlos, Oscar Guillermo, María Angelina Gandolla,
Catherina Perego, Marta Chiodera, Carlo Chiodera) was born on 03 May 1975 in Córdoba,
Argentina. He married INGRID MONICA DELLS. She was born 13 September 1978, in Córdoba,
Argentina.

Lucas Carlos Stiefel and Ingrid Dells had the following child:

i.   THEO CARL STIEFEL DELLS. He was born 6 Febrero 2014 in Barcelona, Spain.

ii.   OLIVIA ANNA STIEFEL DELLS. She was born 8 November 2016 in Barcelona, Spain.

BÁRBARA STIEFEL (Oscar Feliciano Carlos, Oscar Guillermo, María Angelina Gandolla, Catherina Perego, Marta Chiodera, Carlo Chiodera) was born on 14 Jul 1977 in Córdoba, Argentina. She lived with MARIANO ACOSTA.

Mariano Acosta and Bárbara Stiefel had the following child:
i.   TOMÁS ACOSTA was born on 16 Sep 2003 in Córdoba, Argentina.

MARIA TERESA PIZARRO (María Teresa Stiefel, Otto Mario Stiefel, María Angelina Gandolla, Catherina Perego, Marta Chiodera, Carlo Chiodera, Alberto Pizarro). She married ERNESTO A.

Ernesto A and Maria Teresa Pizarro had the following child:
i.   MARÍA SOL A.

MARIA CECILIA PIZARRO (María Teresa Stiefel, Otto Mario Stiefel, María Angelina Gandolla, Catherina Perego, Marta Chiodera, Carlo Chiodera, Alberto Pizarro). She married FERNANDEZ.
Fernandez and Maria Cecilia Pizarro had the following child:
i.   REGINA FERNANDEZ.

RAÚL ANDRÉS Stiefel (Raúl Adolfo, Otto Mario, María Angelina Gandolla, Catherina Perego, Marta Chiodera, Carlo Chiodera) was born on 17 Jun 1962. He married ADRIANA PATRICIA MIANI on 10 Mar 1990. She was born on 19 Sep 1964.

Raúl Andrés Stiefel and Adriana Patricia Miani had the following child:
i.   IGNACIO STIEFEL was born on 28 Apr 1991.

CAROLINA STIEFEL (Raúl Adolfo, Otto Mario, María Angelina Gandolla, Catherina Perego, Marta Chiodera, Carlo Chiodera) was born on 26 Mar 1966. She married JORGE JOFRÉ.

Jorge Jofré and Carolina Stiefel had the following children:
i.   ROCIO JOFRÉ was born on 03 Jan 1996.
ii.   CAROLINA JOFRÉ was born on 04 May 1999.

MARCOS STIEFEL (Raúl Adolfo, Otto Mario, María Angelina Gandolla, Catherina Perego, Marta Chiodera, Carlo Chiodera) was born in 1968. He married PAULA DEL VISO. She was born in 1973.

Marcos Stiefel and Paula del Viso had the following children:
i.   OCTAVIO STIEFEL was born in 2001.
ii.   GREGORIO STIEFEL was born in 2004.
iii.   DIÓGENES STIEFEL was born in 2011.

DIANA STIEFEL (Raúl Adolfo Stiefel, Otto Mario Stiefel, María Angelina Gandolla, Catherina Perego, Marta Chiodera, Carlo Chiodera). She married HORACIO VILLADA.

Horacio Villada and Diana Stiefel had the following children:

i.   HORACIO VILLADA.

ii.   CRUZ VILLADA.

iii.   DIANA VILLADA.

iv.   PAULA VILLADA.

CONSTANZA STIEFEL (Raúl Adolfo Stiefel, Otto Mario Stiefel, María Angelina Gandolla, Catherina Perego, Marta Chiodera, Carlo Chiodera). She married JUAN GNARA.

Juan Gnara and Constanza Stiefel had the following children:

i.   TOMÁS GNARA.

ii.   GASTÓN GNARA.

iii.   SEGUNDO GNARA.

FRANCISCO JOSÉ BECERRA (Beatriz Rita Stiefel, Otto Mario Stiefel, María Angelina Gandolla, Catherina Perego, Marta Chiodera, Carlo Chiodera). He married CONSUELO GUTIERREZ-RIUS.

Francisco José Becerra and Consuelo Gutierrez-Rius had the following children:

i.   FRANCISCO BECERRA.

ii.   ALEJO BECERRA.

iii.   MAGDALENA BECERRA.

iv.   ANGELES BECERRA.

BEATRIZ BECERRA (Beatriz Rita Stiefel, Otto Mario Stiefel, María Angelina Gandolla, Catherina Perego, Marta Chiodera, Carlo Chiodera) was born on 12 Sep 1964. She married LUIS MANZANARES.

Luis Manzanares and Beatriz Becerra had the following children:

i.   CANDELARIA MANZANARES was born on 11 Sep 1989.

ii.   BELEN MANZANARES was born on 06 May 1991.

iii.   PAZ MANZANARES was born on 07 Mar 1992.

iv.   PIA MANZANARES was born on 17 Apr 2000.

SUSANA DEL CARMEN TORRES (Susana Del Carmen Stiefel, Otto Mario Stiefel, María Angelina Gandolla, Catherina Perego, Marta Chiodera, Carlo Chiodera) was born on 30 Oct 1959 in Córdoba, Argentina. She married JUAN CARLOS ALVAREZ.

Juan Carlos Alvarez and Susana del Carmen Torres had the following children:

i.   LUCIO ANDRES ALVAREZ.

ii.   SANTIAGO HERNAN ALVAREZ.

INES MARIA TORRES (Susana Del Carmen Stiefel, Otto Mario Stiefel, María Angelina Gandolla, Catherina Perego, Marta Chiodera, Carlo Chiodera). She married JAVIER NIEVAS.

Javier Nievas and Ines Maria Torres had the following child:
i.   MAURICIO PABLO NIEVAS was born on 08 Mar 1995.

JOSE FRANCISCO TORRES (Susana Del Carmen Stiefel, Otto Mario Stiefel, María Angelina Gandolla, Catherina Perego, Marta Chiodera, Carlo Chiodera) was born on 18 Dec 1963. He married AMY GIL.

Jos Francisco Torres and Amy Gil had the following children:
i.   MARIA MAGDALENA TORRES.
ii.   JOSE AUGUSTO TORRES.
iii.   FRANCISCO MIGUEL TORRES.

MARCELO ORIAS (Noemí Lidia Stiefel, Otto Mario Stiefel, María Angelina Gandolla, Catherina Perego, Marta Chiodera, Carlo Chiodera). He married SUSANA FERRER.

Marcelo Orias and Susana Ferrer had the following children:
i.   CONSTANZA ORIAS was born on 19 May 1989.
ii.   CAROLINA ORIAS was born on 23 Oct 1990.
iii.   CAMILA ORIAS was born on 17 Feb 1994.
iv.   AGUSTÍN ORIAS was born on 05 Nov 1995.

VALERIA M. STIEFEL (Otto Carlos Stiefel, Otto Mario Stiefel, María Angelina Gandolla, Catherina Perego, Marta Chiodera, Carlo Chiodera). She married GUSTAVO CROSETTO.

Gustavo Crosetto and Valeria M. Stiefel had the following children
i.   PAULA VICTORIA CROSETTO
ii.   AGUSTÍN CROSETTO.
iii.   MARÍA CANDELARIA CROSETTO.

LUCRECIA STIEFEL (Otto Carlos Stiefel, Otto Mario Stiefel, María Angelina Gandolla, Catherina Perego, Marta Chiodera, Carlo Chiodera). She married GUSTAVO YUNES.

Gustavo Yunes and Lucrecia Stiefel had the following children:
i.   ELIAS MANUEL YUNES.
ii.   TOMÁS JOAQUÍN YUNES.
iii.   LUCAS GUSTAVO YUNES.
iv.   MATEO JOSÉ YUNES.
v.   LUCÍA VICTORIA YUNES.

JOSEFINA STIEFEL (Otto Carlos Stiefel, Otto Mario Stiefel, María Angelina Gandolla, Catherina Perego, Marta Chiodera, Carlo Chiodera) She married JOSÉ MANUEL GARCIA on 30 Apr 1999.

José Manuel Garcia and Josefina Stiefel had the following children:

i.   IGNACIO OTTO GARCIA was born on 12 Apr 2006.
ii.   JOAQUÍN JOSÉ GARCIA was born on 08 Aug 2008.

MAGDALENA GORROCHATEGUI (María Luisa Stiefel, Otto Mario Stiefel, María Angelina Gandolla, Catherina Perego, Marta Chiodera, Carlo Chiodera) was born on 01 Jan 1969. She married PABLO REVOLA.

Pablo Revola and Magdalena Gorrochategui had the following children:

i.   MARIO REVOLA.
ii.   MARTINA REVOLA.

CELINA GORROCHATEGUI (María Luisa Stiefel, Otto Mario Stiefel, María Angelina Gandolla, Catherina Perego, Marta Chiodera, Carlo Chiodera) was born on 13 Mar 1970. She married OSCAR RUIZ LUQUE.

Oscar Ruiz Luque and Celina Gorrochategui had the following children:

i.   PILAR LUQUE.
ii.   JUSTINA LUQUE

ESTEBAN GORROCHATEGUI (María Luisa Stiefel, Otto Mario Stiefel, María Angelina Gandolla, Catherina Perego, Marta Chiodera, Carlo Chiodera) was born on 25 Feb 1971. He married CONSUELO NORES.

Esteban Gorrochategui and Consuelo Nores had the following children:

i.   CRUZ GORROCHATEGUI.
ii.   FACUNDO GORROCHATEGUI.

INES GORROCHATEGUI (María Luisa Stiefel, Otto Mario Stiefel, María Angelina Gandolla, Catherina Perego, Marta Chiodera, Carlo Chiodera) was born on 13 Jun 1973. She married GUSTAVO OLIVA.

Gustavo Oliva and Ines Gorrochategui had the following children:

i.   LUCA OLIVA.
ii.   EMMA OLIVA.

Generation 8

ZEYA XOCHITL AYEZ (Kenya Clavel Ayez, Carlos Cuauhtemoc Ayala, Marta Beatriz Catalina Stiefel, Oscar Guillermo Stiefel, María Angelina Gandolla, Catherina Perego, Marta Chiodera, Carlo Chiodera) was born 11 November 2021 at 6:50 am in Santa Rosa, California. She was 7 lb 9 oz and 20.5 inches long. This day was Indigenous People's Day, Canadian Thanksgiving Day, International Day of the Girl Child. She arrived in time to be welcomed into the world by her father, Anthony, grandparents, Mary Ann and Carlos, and her Aunt Maya (who thankfully had the day off work).

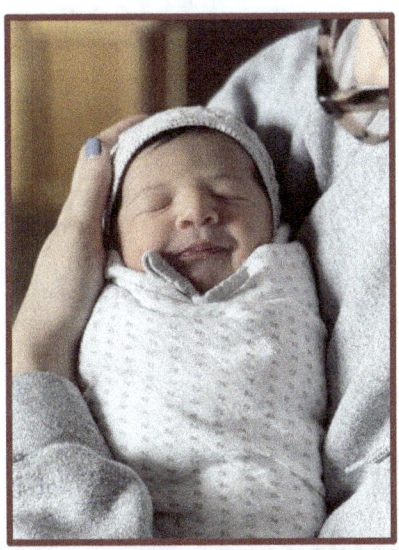

Four generations: Marta, Carlos, Kenya, and baby Zeya

91

FamilySearch™ International Genealogical Index v5.0

Southwest Europe

Family Group Record

Husband
  Angelo GANDOLA

Pedigree

  Birth: < 1815> <Bellagio, Como, Italy>
  Christening:
  Marriage: < 1840> <Bellagio, Como, Italy>
  Death:
  Burial:

Wife
  Angela Maria CURIONI

Pedigree

  Birth: < 1819> <Bellagio, Como, Italy>
  Christening:
  Marriage: < 1840> <Bellagio, Como, Italy>
  Death:
  Burial:

Children

---

1. Domenico Enrico GANDOLA CURIONI
   Male

Pedigree

   Birth: 27 MAR 1841 Bellagio, Como, Italy
   Christening:
   Death: 11 FEB 1908
   Burial:

---

2. Aristides GANDOLA CURIONI
   Male

Pedigree

   Birth: < 1843> <Bellagio, Como, Italy>
   Christening:
   Death:
   Burial:

---

3. Maria GANDOLA CURIONI
   Female

Pedigree

   Birth: < 1845> <Bellagio, Como, Italy>
   Christening:
   Death:
   Burial:

---

http://www.familysearch.org/eng/search/IGI/family_group_record.asp?familyid=26500690... 8/29/2009

FamilySearch™ International Genealogical Index v5.0

Southwest Europe

Family Group Record

Husband
Domenico Enrico GANDOLA CURIONI

Pedigree

Birth: 27 MAR 1841 Bellagio, Como, Italy
Christening:
Marriage: 07 MAR 1872 Rosario, Santa Fe, Argentina
Death: 11 FEB 1908
Burial:

Wife
Margarita GRANT ROSS

Pedigree

Birth: 20 FEB 1837 <Rosario, Santa Fe, Argentina>
Christening:
Marriage: 07 MAR 1872 Rosario, Santa Fe, Argentina
Death: 13 APR 1922
Burial:

Father: Alejandro GRANT
Mother: Maria ROSS

Family

Children

1. Emma GANDOLLA GRANT
   Female

   Pedigree

   Birth: 29 NOV 1872 Rosario, Santa Fe, Argentina
   Christening:
   Death:
   Burial:

---

2. Arturo GANDOLLA GRANT
   Male

   Pedigree

   Birth: 08 OCT 1877 Rosario, Santa Fe, Argentina
   Christening:
   Death: 18 SEP 1937
   Burial:

---

3. Unavailable

Pedigree

FamilySearch™ International Genealogical Index v5.0

South America

Family Group Record

Husband
Rafael JIMENO   Pedigree

Birth: 21 APR 1868 <Rosario, Santa Fe, Argentina>
Christening:
Marriage: 25 JUL 1896 Rosario, Santa Fe, Argentina
Death: 06 JUN 1941
Burial:

Wife
Emma GANDOLLA GRANT   Pedigree

Birth: 29 NOV 1872 Rosario, Santa Fe, Argentina
Christening:
Marriage: 25 JUL 1896 Rosario, Santa Fe, Argentina
Death:
Burial:

Children

---

1. Rafael JIMENO GANDOLLA   Pedigree
   Male

   Birth: 20 MAR 1897 Rosario, Santa Fe, Argentina
   Christening:
   Death:
   Burial:

---

2. Ernesto JIMENO GANDOLLA   Pedigree
   Male

   Birth: 17 AUG 1898 Rosario, Santa Fe, Argentina
   Christening:
   Death:
   Burial:

---

3. Enrique JIMENO GANDOLLA   Pedigree
   Male

   Birth: 21 MAR 1900 Rosario, Santa Fe, Argentina
   Christening:
   Death:
   Burial:

---

4. Emma Margarita JIMENO GANDOLLA   Pedigree
   Female

   Birth: 16 MAR 1902 Rosario, Santa Fe, Argentina
   Christening:
   Death: 03 JAN 1903
   Burial:

59
http://www.familysearch.org/eng/search/IGI/family_group_record.asp?familyid=2650069... 10/27/2009

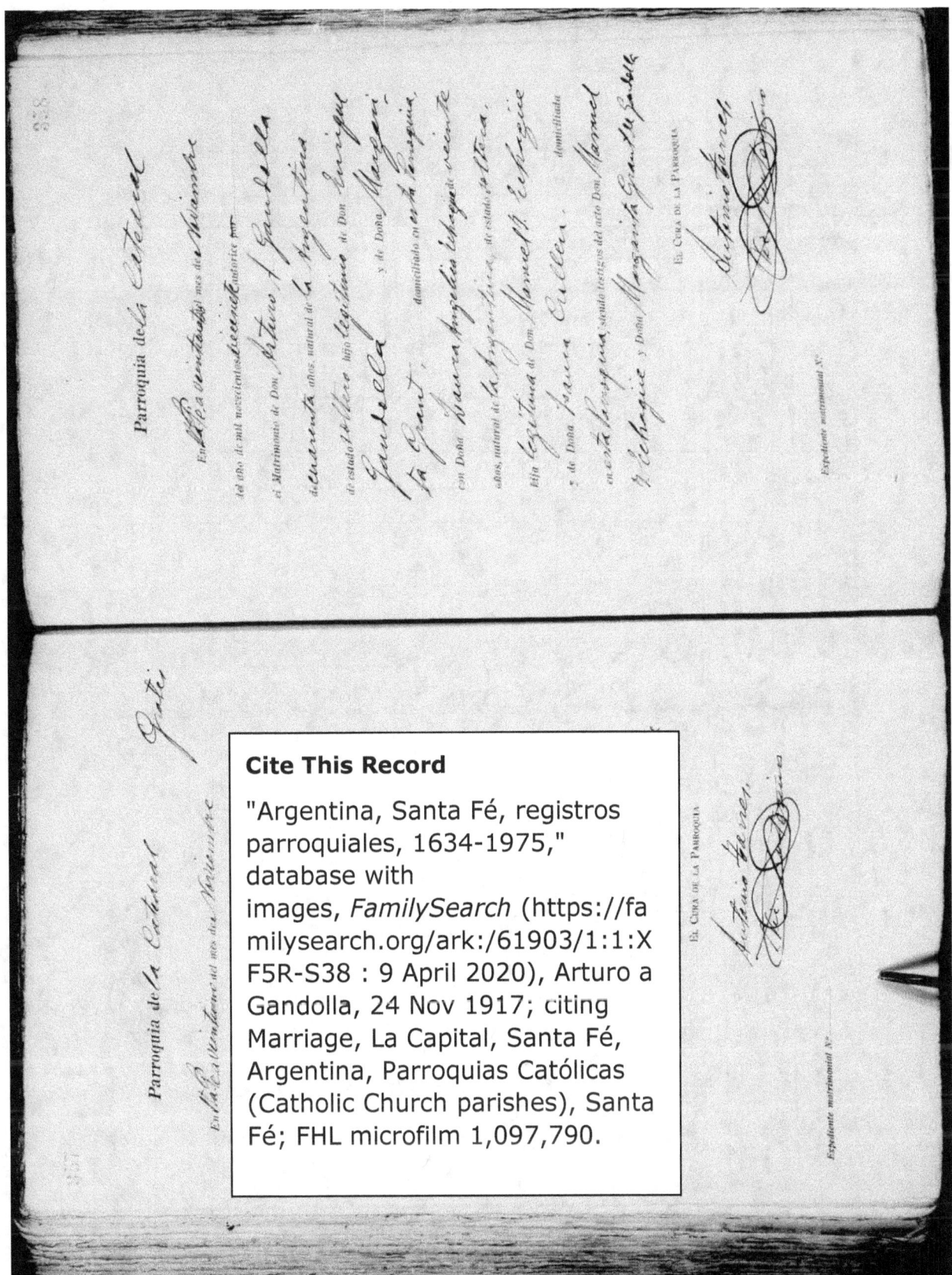

Cite This Record

"Argentina, Santa Fé, registros parroquiales, 1634-1975," database with images, *FamilySearch* (https://familysearch.org/ark:/61903/1:1:XF5R-S38 : 9 April 2020), Arturo a Gandolla, 24 Nov 1917; citing Marriage, La Capital, Santa Fé, Argentina, Parroquias Católicas (Catholic Church parishes), Santa Fé; FHL microfilm 1,097,790.

Sección 1 de S. Martín

Boletín para un hogar ó familia

Orden	CUAL ES SU APELLIDO? NOMBRE?	Es varón ó mujer	Cuantos años ha cumplido	Es soltero, casado ó viudo	A qué nación pertenece	Si es argentino, provincia ó ... donde ha nacido	Qué profesión, oficio, ocupación ó medio de vida tiene	Sabe leer y escribir	Vá á la escuela	Posee la propie-dad raíz	SI ES MUJER CASADA ó VIUDA — Cuantos hijos ha tenido / Cuantos años de matrimonio tiene	Es enfermo, sordo-mudo, idiota, loco ó ciego	Tiene bocio ó coto	INVÁLIDO Por guerra	Por acci-dente	Huérfano de padre y madre
1	Castillo Enrique	varon	35	casado	Italiana		albañil	si								
2	Giro? Margarita	mujer	30	casada	Argentina	Buenos Aires	costurera	si								
3	Castillo Francisco	varon	22	soltero	Argentina	Santa Fe	albañil	si								
4	Castillo Enrique	varon	20	soltero	Argentina	Santa Fe		si								
5	Juan Castillo	mujer	13	soltera	Argentina	Santa Fe		si								
6	Bianchi Eugenio	varon	30	soltero	Italiana		comerciante	si							de padre
7	Rómolo ... africana	mujer	19	soltera	Argentina	Santa Fe		si							de madre
8	... Rosario	varon	12	soltero	Argentina	Santa Fe		si								

EMPADRONADOR Gregorio Bergamaschi

ABUELA MARIA BAPTISMAL RECORD

Name **Angela Maria Marta Gandolla**
Sex **Female**
Christening Date **17 Aug 1878**
Christening Place **Rosario, Santa Fé, Argentina**
Father's Name **Aristides Gandoll**a
Father's Sex **Male**
Mother's Name **Catalina Peregó**
Mother's Sex **Female**

"Argentina bautismos, 1645-1930",
database, *FamilySearch* (https://familysearch.org/ark:/61903/1:1:XNBK-HHK: 13 February 2020),
Angela Maria Marta Gandolla, 1878.

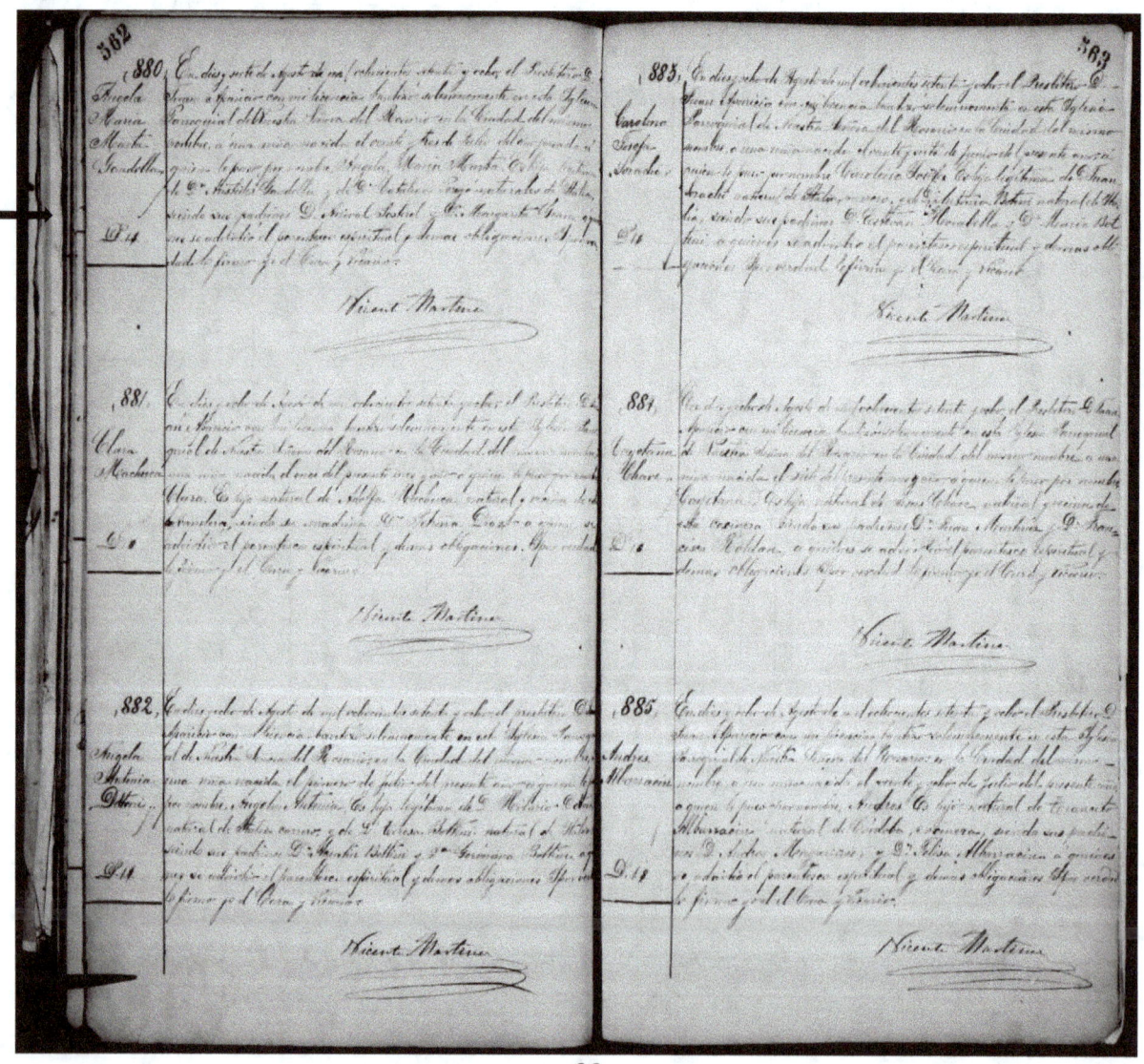

MARRIAGE OF ARISTADES AND CATALINA

174-1998 **Event** Place Note
Name **Arístides Gandolla**
Sex **Male** Age: **31**
Birth Year (Estimated) **1845**
Father's Name **Angel Gandolla**
Mother's Name **Maria Cúriona**
Spouse's Name **Catalina Perego**
Spouse's Sex **Female** Spouse's Age **26**
Spouse's Birth Year (Estimated)**1850**
Spouse's Father's Name **Juan Perego**
Spouse's Mother's Name **Maria Cheodera**
Marriage Date **6 Aug 1876**
Marriage Place **Nuestra Señora del Rosario, Rosario, Santa Fé, Argentina**

"Argentina, Santa Fé, registros parroquiales, 1634-1975," database with
images, *FamilySearch* (https://familysearch.org/ark:/61903/1:1:QGX6-T6HK: 9 April 2020),
Arístides Gandolla, 6 Aug 1876; citing Marriage, Nuestra Señora del Rosario, Rosario, Rosario,
Santa Fé, Argentina, Parroquias Católicas (Catholic Church parishes), Santa Fé; FHL microfilm.

PHOTOS FROM RIO DEL MEDIO SHOWING HOUSE, RIVER, CEMETERY, AND
TOMBS OF ABUELA MARIA, ABUELO CARLOS, AND AUNTS AND UNCLES

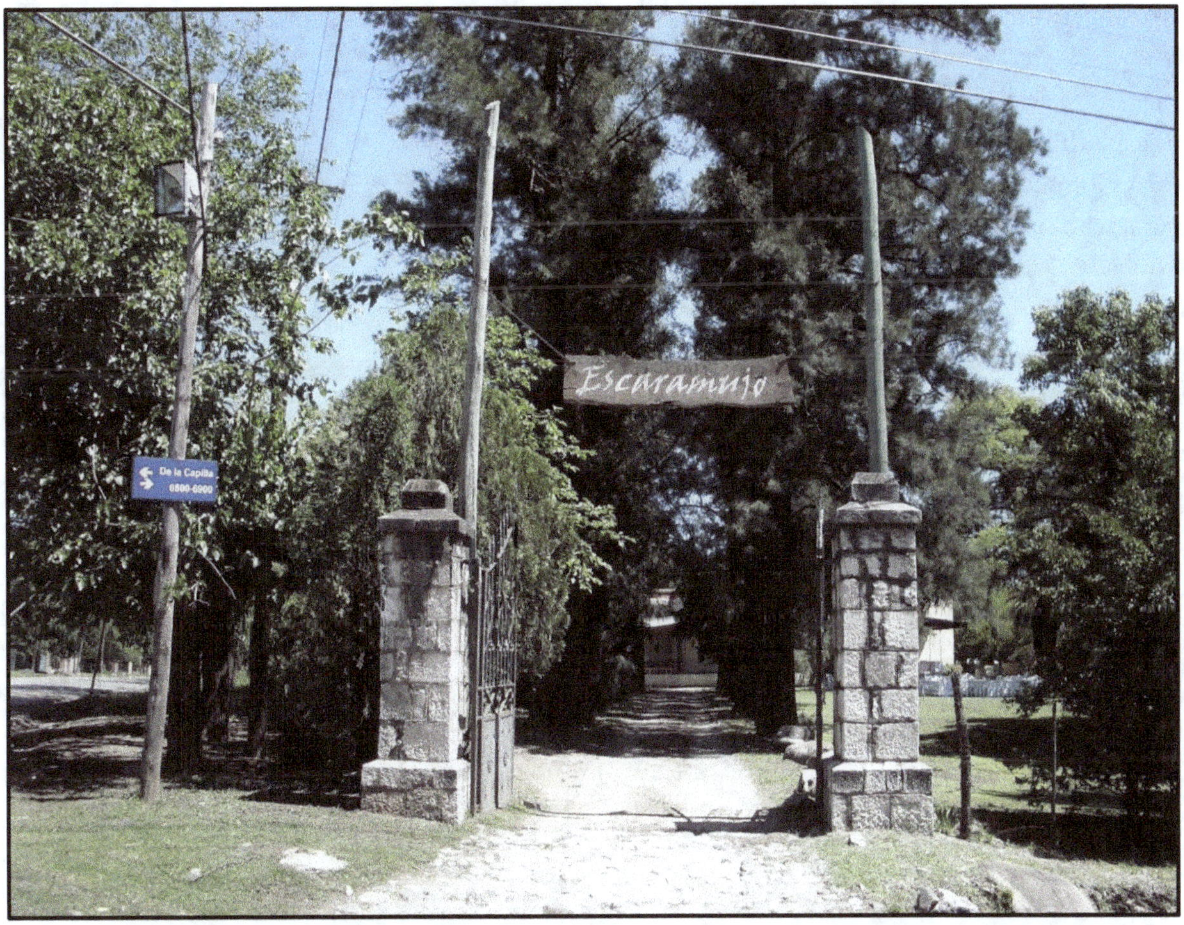
Escaramujo
De la Capilla

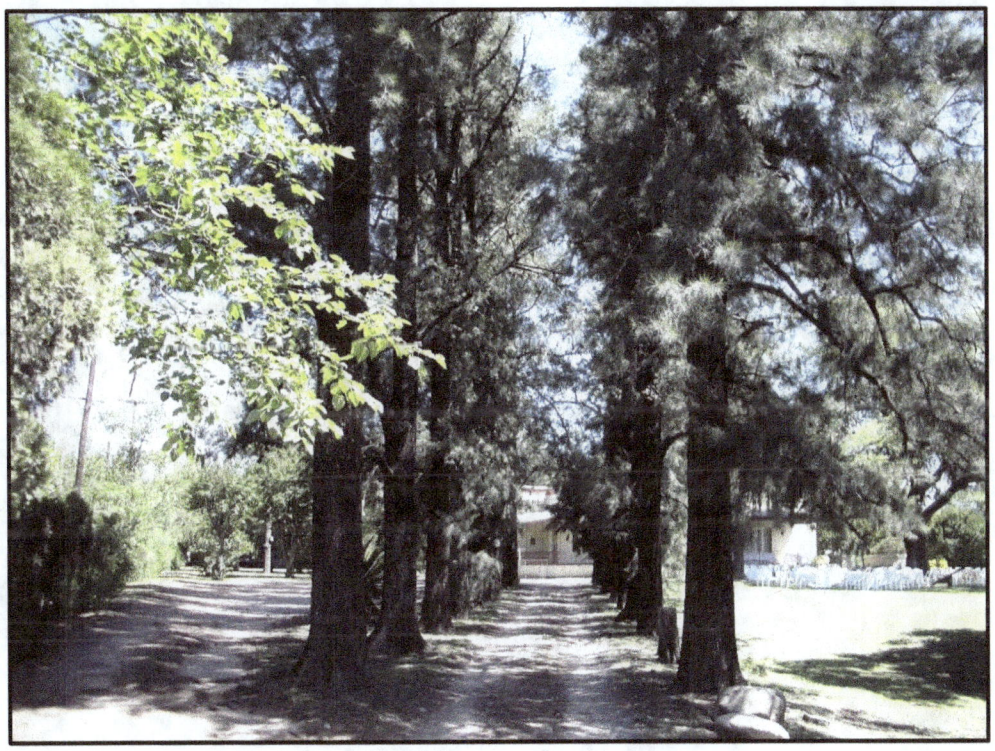

DEDICATION

I dedicate this book to my cousin,
Susana González-Albarracín, better known as
Tatana, who passed away on February 8, 2022, in
Córdoba, Argentina, of COVID-19 complications.
She was a major force in our genealogy quest.
She spent many hours on the phone and on the
internet, looking for missing relatives, encouraging
people to attend our family reunions, and in
general, connecting members of the family
together. Her "Pandora Suitcase," full of old family
photos, opened a whole world of new relatives we
did not know existed. She was quick to smile and
found the funny side of everything.
She will be greatly missed!

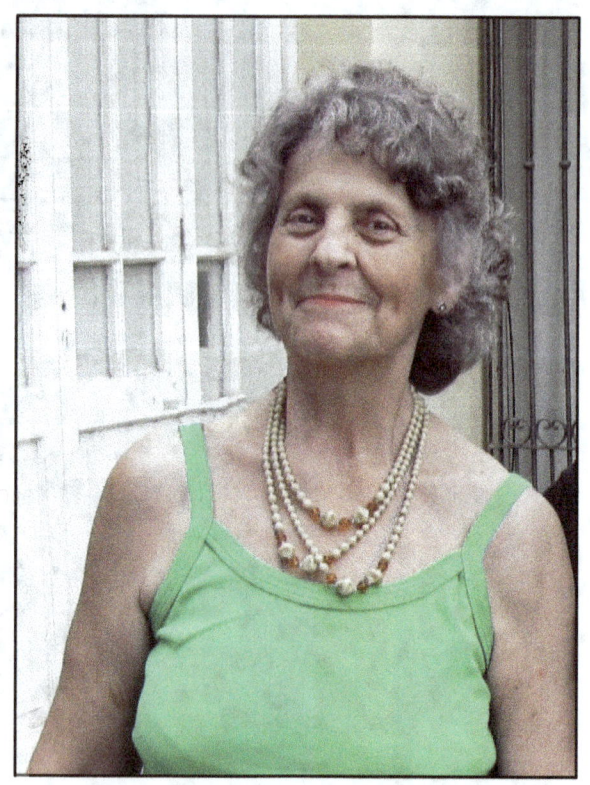

ACKNOWLEDGEMENT

I would like to express my most heartfelt thanks to
Catherine "Cat" Shehan Ayala, who spent many
hours editing this document. Her expertise, patience,
and sense of order made this a much better book!
Cat, I could not have done it without you. Thank
you for taking this project seriously.